THE KEY

STUDENT STUDY GUIDE

12 Calculus and Vectors
rsity Preparation (MCV4U)

THE KEY student study guide is designed to help students achieve success in school. The content in each study guide is 100% curriculum aligned and serves as an excellent source of material for review and practice. To create this book, teachers, curriculum specialists, and assessment experts have worked closely to develop the instructional pieces that explain each of the key concepts for the course. The practice questions and sample tests have detailed solutions that show problem-solving methods, highlight concepts that are likely to be tested, and point out potential sources of errors. ***THE KEY*** is a complete guide to be used by students throughout the school year for reviewing and understanding course content, and to prepare for assessments.

Rao,Gautam,1961 –
THE KEY – Math 12 - Calculus and Vectors Ontario

1. Mathematics – Juvenile Literature. I. Title

Castle Rock Research Corporation
2340 Manulife Place
10180 – 101 Street
Edmonton, AB T5J 3S4

1 2 3 FP 13 12 11

Publisher
Gautam Rao

Contributors
Bob Frizzell
Renee Nutt
Tyler Starr Crawford
Victoria Garlitos

CASTLE ROCK
RESEARCH CORP

Dedicated to the memory of Dr. V. S. Rao

THE KEY–Math 12 Calculus and Vectors

THE KEY consists of the following sections:

KEY Tips for Being Successful at School gives examples of study and review strategies. It includes information about learning styles, study schedules, and note taking for test preparation.

Class Focus includes a unit on each area of the curriculum. Units are divided into sections, each focusing on one of the specific expectations, or main ideas, that students must learn about in that unit. Examples, definitions, and visuals help to explain each main idea. Practice questions on the main ideas are also included. At the end of each unit is a test on the important ideas covered. The practice questions and unit tests help students identify areas they know and those they need to study more. They can also be used as preparation for tests and quizzes. Most questions are of average difficulty, though some are easy and some are hard—the harder questions are called *Challenger Questions*. Each unit is prefaced by a ***Table of Correlations***, which correlates questions in the unit to the specific curriculum expectations. Answers and solutions are found at the end of each unit.

KEY Strategies for Success on Tests helps students get ready for tests. It shows students different types of questions they might see, word clues to look for when reading them, and hints for answering them.

Practice Tests includes one to three tests based on the entire course. They are very similar to the format and level of difficulty that students may encounter on final tests. In some regions, these tests may be reprinted versions of official tests, or reflect the same difficulty levels and formats as official versions. This gives students the chance to practice using real-world examples. Answers and complete solutions are provided at the end of the section.

For the complete curriculum document (including specific expectations along with examples and sample problems), visit www.edu.gov.on.ca/eng/curriculum/secondary.

THE KEY *Study Guides* are available for many courses. Check www.castlerockresearch.com for a complete listing of books available for your area.

For information about any of our resources or services, please call Castle Rock Research at 905.625.3332 or visit our website at http://www.castlerockresearch.com.

At Castle Rock Research, we strive to produce an error-free resource. If you should find an error, please contact us so that future editions can be corrected.

CONTENTS

KEY Tips for Being Successful at School

KEY TIPS FOR BEING SUCCESSFUL AT SCHOOL

KEY FACTORS CONTRIBUTING TO SCHOOL SUCCESS

In addition to learning the content of your courses, there are some other things that you can do to help you do your best at school. Some of these strategies are listed below.

- **Keep a positive attitude:** Always reflect on what you can already do and what you already know.
- **Be prepared to learn**: Have ready the necessary pencils, pens, notebooks, and other required materials for participating in class.
- **Complete all of your assignments:** Do your best to finish all of your assignments. Even if you know the material well, practice will reinforce your knowledge. If an assignment or question is difficult for you, work through it as far as you can so that your teacher can see exactly where you are having difficulty.
- **Set small goals for yourself when you are learning new material:** For example, when learning the parts of speech, do not try to learn everything in one night. Work on only one part or section each study session. When you have memorized one particular part of speech and understand it, then move on to another one, continue this process until you have memorized and learned all the parts of speech.
- **Review your classroom work regularly at home:** Review to be sure that you understand the material that you learned in class.
- **Ask your teacher for help**: Your teacher will help you if you do not understand something or if you are having a difficult time completing your assignments.
- **Get plenty of rest and exercise:** Concentrating in class is hard work. It is important to be well-rested and have time to relax and socialize with your friends. This helps you to keep your positive attitude about your school work.
- **Eat healthy meals:** A balanced diet keeps you healthy and gives you the energy that you need for studying at school and at home.

How To Find Your Learning Style

Every student learns differently. The manner in which you learn best is called your learning style. By knowing your learning style, you can increase your success at school. Most students use a combination of learning styles. Do you know what type of learner you are? Read the following descriptions. Which of these common learning styles do you use most often?

- **Linguistic Learner**: You may learn best by saying, hearing, and seeing words. You are probably really good at memorizing things such as dates, places, names, and facts. You may need **to write and then say out loud** the steps in a process, a formula, or the actions that lead up to a significant event.

- **Spatial Learner**: You may learn best by looking at and working with pictures. You are probably really good at puzzles, imagining things, and reading maps and charts. You may need to use strategies like **mind mapping and webbing** to organize your information and study notes.

- **Kinaesthetic Learner**: You may learn best by touching, moving, and figuring things out using manipulative. You are probably really good at physical activities and learning through movement. You may need to **draw your finger over a diagram** to remember it, **"tap out" the steps** needed to solve a problem, or **"feel" yourself writing** or typing a formula.

Scheduling Study Time

You should review your class notes regularly to ensure that you have a clear understanding of all the new material you learned. Reviewing your lessons on a regular basis helps you to learn and remember ideas and concepts. It also reduces the quantity of material that you need to study prior to a test. Establishing a study schedule will help you to make the best use of your time.

Regardless of the type of study schedule you use, you may want to consider the following suggestions to maximize your study time and effort:

- Organize your work so that you begin with the most challenging material first.
- Divide the subject's content into small, manageable chunks.
- Alternate regularly between your different subjects and types of study activities in order to maintain your interest and motivation.
- Make a daily list with headings like "Must Do," "Should Do," and "Could Do."
- Begin each study session by quickly reviewing what you studied the day before.
- Maintain your usual routine of eating, sleeping, and exercising to help you concentrate better for extended periods of time.

CREATING STUDY NOTES

MIND-MAPPING OR WEBBING

Use the key words, ideas, or concepts from your reading or class notes to create a *mind map* or *web* (a diagram or visual representation of the given information). A mind map or web is sometimes referred to as a knowledge map.

- Write the key word, concept, theory, or formula in the centre of your page.
- Write down related facts, ideas, events, and information and then link them to the central concept with lines.
- Use coloured markers, underlining, or other symbols to emphasize things such as relationships, time lines, and important information.

The following examples of a Frayer Model illustrate how this technique can be used to study mathematical vocabulary.

Perimeter

Definition – Perimeter is the distance around a polygon	**Characteristics** – Measured in linear units (e.g., metres, centimetres)
Examples – Fence around a yard – Distance around a circle (circumference)	**Non-examples** – Grass covering a yard – Area of rug covering a floor

Cube

Definition A cube is a solid 3-D object that has – 6 square faces, all equal in size – 8 vertices – 12 equal edges	**Visual Presentation** 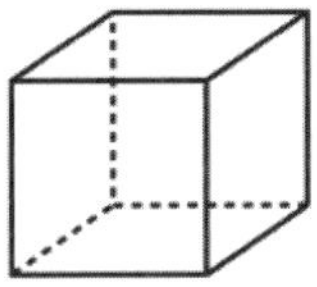
Characteristics or Properties – 6 square faces – 8 vertices – 12 edges – 6 flat faces	**Examples** 

INDEX CARDS

To use index cards while studying, follow these steps:

- Write a key word or question on one side of an index card.
- On the reverse side, write the definition of the word, answer to the question, or any other important information that you want to remember.

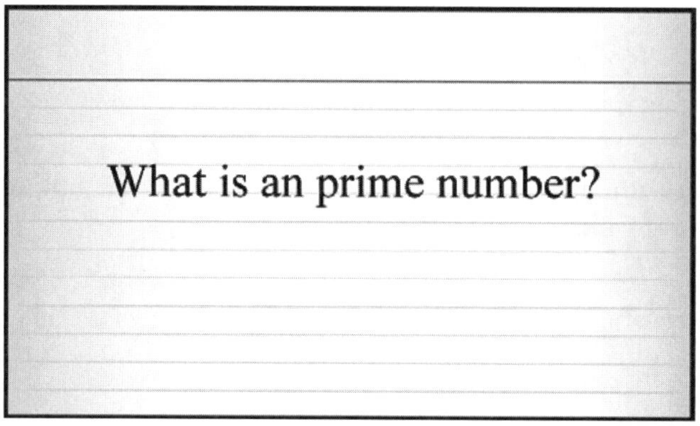

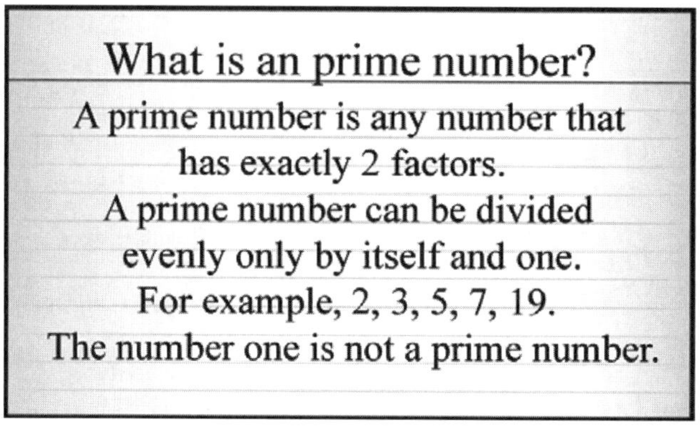

SYMBOLS AND STICKY NOTES—IDENTIFYING IMPORTANT INFORMATION

- Use symbols to mark your class notes. For example, an exclamation mark (!) might be used to point out something that must be learned well because it is a very important idea. A question mark (?) may highlight something that you are not certain about, and a diamond (◊) or asterisk (*) could highlight interesting information that you want to remember.
- Use sticky notes when you are not allowed to put marks in books.
- Use sticky notes to mark a page in a book that contains an important diagram, formula, explanation, etc.
- Use sticky notes to mark important facts in research books.

Memorization Techniques

- **Association** relates new learning to something you already know. For example, to remember the spelling difference between *dessert* and *desert*, recall that the word *sand* has only one *s*. So, because there is sand in a desert, the word *desert* only has on *s*.
- **Mnemonic** devices are sentences that you create to remember a list or group of items. For example, the first letter of each word in the phrase "**E**very **G**ood **B**oy **D**eserves **F**udge" helps you to remember the names of the lines on the treble clef staff (E, G, B, D, and F) in music.
- **Acronyms** are words that are formed from the first letters or parts of the words in a group. For example, **RADAR** is actually an acronym for **Ra**dio **D**etecting **A**nd **R**anging, and **MASH** is an acronym for **M**obile **A**rmy **S**urgical **H**ospital. **HOMES** helps you to remember the names of the five Great Lakes (**H**uron, **O**ntario, **M**ichigan, **E**rie, and **S**uperior).
- **Visualizing** requires you to use your mind's eye to "see" a chart, list, map, diagram, or sentence as it is in your textbook or notes, on the chalk board or computer screen, or in a display.
- **Initialisms** are abbreviations that are formed from the first letters or parts of the words in a group. Unlike acronyms, initialisms cannot be pronounced as a word themselves. For example, **BEDMAS** is an initialism for the order of operations in math (**B**rackets, **E**xponents, **D**ivide, **M**ultiply, **A**dd, **S**ubtract).

Key Strategies for Reviewing

Reviewing textbook material, class notes, and handouts should be an ongoing activity. Spending time reviewing becomes more critical when you are preparing for tests. You may find some of the following review strategies useful when studying during your scheduled study time.

- Before reading a selection, preview it by noting the headings, charts, graphs, and chapter questions.
- Read the complete introduction to identify the key information that is addressed in the selection.
- Read the first sentence of the next paragraph for the main idea.
- Skim the paragraph and note the key words, phrases, and information.
- Read the last sentence of the paragraph.
- Repeat this process for each paragraph and section until you have skimmed the entire selection.

KEY Strategies for Success: A Checklist

Review, review, review: review is a huge part of doing well at school and preparing for tests. Here is a checklist for you to keep track of how many suggested strategies for success you are using. Read each question and then put a check mark (✓) in the correct column. Look at the questions where you have checked the "No" column. Think about how you might try using some of these strategies to help you do your best at school.

***KEY* Strategies for Success**	**Yes**	**No**
Do you attend school regularly?		
Do you know your personal learning style—how you learn best?		
Do you spend 15 to 30 minutes a day reviewing your notes?		
Do you study in a quiet place at home?		
Do you clearly mark the most important ideas in your study notes?		
Do you use sticky notes to mark texts and research books?		
Do you practise answering multiple-choice and written-response questions?		
Do you ask your teacher for help when you need it?		
Are you maintaining a healthy diet and sleep routine?		
Are you participating in regular physical activity?		

Rate of Change

Rate of Change

Table of Correlations

	Outcome	Practice Questions	Unit Test Questions	Practice Test 1	Practice Test 2
RC1.0	Investigating Instantaneous Rate of Change at a Point				
RC1.1	*describe examples of real-world applications of rates of change, represented in a variety of ways*	1, 2	1, 2		1
RC1.2	*describe connections between the average rate of change of a function that is smooth (i.e., continuous with no corners) over an interval and the slope of the corresponding secant, and between the instantaneous rate of change of a smooth function at a point and the slope of the tangent at that point*	3, 4	3, 4	1	2
RC1.3	*make connections, with or without graphing technology, between an approximate value of the instantaneous rate of change at a given point on the graph of a smooth function and average rates of change over intervals containing the point (i.e., by using secants through the given point on a smooth curve to approach the tangent at that point, and determining the slopes of the approaching secants to approximate the slope of the tangent)*	5, 6	5, 6	2	
RC1.4	*recognize, through investigation with or without technology, graphical and numerical examples of limits, and explain the reasoning involved*	7	7		3
RC1.5	*make connections, for a function that is smooth over the interval a [lesser than or equal to symbol] x [lesser than or equal to symbol] a + h, between the average rate of change of the function over this interval and the value of the expression f(a + h) – f(a)/h , and between the instantaneous rate of change of the function at x = a and the value of the limit lim[h arrow 0] f(a + h) – f(a)/h*	8, 9	8, 9	3	4
RC1.6	*compare, through investigation, the calculation of instantaneous rates of change at a point (a, f(a)) for polynomial functions, with and without f(a + h) – f(a)/h simplifying the expression before substituting values of that approach zero*	10, 11	10, 11	4	5
RC2.0	Investigating the Concept of the Derivative Function				
RC2.1	*determine numerically and graphically the intervals over which the instantaneous rate of change is positive, negative, or zero for a function that is smooth over these intervals (e.g., by using graphing technology to examine the table of values and the slopes of tangents for a function whose equation is given; by examining a given graph), and describe the behaviour of the instantaneous rate of change at and between local maxima and minima*	12, 13, 14	12, 13, 14	5, 6	6
RC2.2	*generate, through investigation using technology, a table of values showing the instantaneous rate of change of a polynomial function, f(x), for various values of x (e.g., construct a tangent to the function, measure its slope, and create a slider or animation to move the point of tangency), graph the ordered pairs, recognize that the graph represents a function called the derivative, f′(x) or dy/dx, and make connections between the graphs of f(x) and f′(x) or y and dy/dx [e.g., when f(x) is linear, f′(x) is constant; when f(x) is quadratic, f′(x) is linear; when f(x) is cubic, f′(x) is quadratic]*	15	15		

RC2.3	*determine the derivatives of polynomial functions by simplifying the algebraic expression f(x + h) – f(x)/h and then taking the limit of the simplified expression as h approaches zero [i.e., determining lim[h arrow 0] f(x + h) – f(x)/h]*	16, 17	16, 17	7	7
RC2.4	*determine, through investigation using technology, the graph of the derivative f′(x)or dy of a given sinusoidal function [i.e., dx f(x) = sin x, f(x) = cos x] (e.g., by generating a table of values showing the instantaneous rate of change of the function for various values of x and graphing the ordered pairs; by using dynamic geometry software to verify graphically that when f(x) = sin x, f′(x) = cos x, and when f(x) = cos x, f′(x) = –sin x; by using a motion sensor to compare the displacement and velocity of a pendulum)*	18	18, 19		
RC2.5	*determine, through investigation using technology, the graph of the derivative f′(x)or dy/dx of a given exponential function [i.e., f(x) = a(x) (a > 0, a ≠ 1)], and make connections between the graphs of f(x) and f′(x) or y and dy/dx*	19, 20	20, 21		8
RC2.6	*determine, through investigation using technology, the exponential function f(x) = a(x) (a > 0, a ≠ 1) for which f′(x) = f(x) (e.g., by using graphing technology to create a slider that varies the value of a in order to determine the exponential function whose graph is the same as the graph of its derivative), identify the number e to be the value of a for which f′(x) = f(x) [i.e., given f(x) = e(x), f (x) = e(x)], and recognize that for the exponential function f(x) = e(x) the slope of the tangent at any point on the function is equal to the value of the function at that point*	21	22	8	9
RC2.7	*recognize that the natural logarithmic function f(x) = log(e)x, also written as f(x) = ln x, is the inverse of the exponential function f(x) = e(x), and make connections between f(x) = ln x and f(x) = e(x)*	22	23	9	10
RC2.8	*verify, using technology (e.g., calculator, graphing technology), that the derivative of the exponential function f(x) = a(x) is f′(x) = ax ln a for various values of a*	23	24	10, 11	11
RC3.0	Investigating the Properties of Derivatives				
RC3.1	*verify the power rule for functions of the form f(x) = x(n), where n is a natural number*	24	25	12	12
RC3.2	*verify the constant, constant multiple, sum, and difference rules graphically and numerically, and read and interpret proofs involving lim[h arrow 0] f(x + h) – f(x)/h of the constant, constant multiple, sum, and difference rules (student reproduction of the development of the general case is not required)*	25, 26	26, 36	13	13
RC3.3	*determine algebraically the derivatives of polynomial functions, and use these derivatives to determine the instantaneous rate of change at a point and to determine point(s) at which a given rate of change occurs*	27, 28, 29, 30	27, 28, 29, 37	14	14
RC3.4	*verify that the power rule applies to functions of the form f(x) = x(n), where n is a rational number, and verify algebraically the chain rule using monomial functions and the product rule using polynomial functions*	31	30	15	15
RC3.5	*solve problems, using the product and chain rules, involving the derivatives of polynomial functions, sinusoidal functions, exponential functions, rational functions, radical functions, and other simple combinations of functions**	32, 33, 34, 35, 36	31, 32, 33, 34, 35	16	16

RC1.1 describe examples of real-world applications of rates of change, represented in a variety of ways

Applications of Rates of Change

There are numerous applications and situations involving rate of change.

With the present-day interest in global warming, there are many historical studies and a lot of research being done on the rate at which various regions of Earth are warming. On a related topic, there is research on how fast the ozone layer of the atmosphere is being depleted.

In medicine, there are studies on the rate of advancement of disease, and the rate of effectiveness of drugs and other treatments.

In finance and economics, there is interest in many rates of change, such as the rate of growth of economies and the rate of change of the values of stock markets.

The rate of change of displacement with respect to time is called velocity. When an object is dropped from a height of 200 m, its velocity, v, in metres per second, toward the centre of Earth after t seconds is given by the formula $v = -9.8t$. This formula disregards the effect of air friction on the object. Thus, after 3 s, the velocity of the object is $v = -9.8(3) = -29.4$. The negative sign indicates the direction is toward Earth rather than away from it.

Graphs are often used to show or emphasize rates of change. For example, consider what happens to the temperature in a barbecue when it is turned off.

This graph shows the temperature, y (measured in degrees Celsius), in a particular barbecue x minutes after it has been turned off.

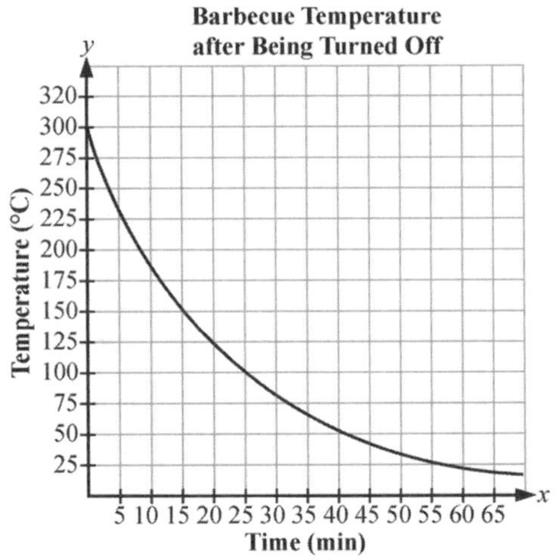

The temperature of the barbecue falls quickly initially (the graph is steep) and much more slowly as time passes (the graph is getting flatter). This shows that the rate of change of the temperature with respect to time is greater initially (negatively) than it is after it gets closer to the temperature of the surrounding air.

1. Which of the following changes does **not** represent a positive rate of change?

A. The change in temperature of water being heated over time

B. The change in fuel economy as a vehicle increases its speed

C. The change in tension of a spring as the spring is compressed

D. The change in average monthly temperature in Canada from January to May

Use the following information to answer the next question.

> An object's position, s, in metres with respect to time, t, in seconds is given by the formula $s = 2t - 5$.

2. What is the rate of change of the object from 0 to 5 s?

A. 0.0 m/s   **B.** 2.0 m/s

C. 2.5 m/s   **D.** 5.0 m/s

RC1.2 describe connections between the average rate of change of a function that is smooth (i.e., continuous with no corners) over an interval and the slope of the corresponding secant, and between the instantaneous rate of change of a smooth function at a point and the slope of the tangent at that point

UNDERSTANDING AVERAGE RATE OF CHANGE AND INSTANTANEOUS RATE OF CHANGE

The **average rate of change** of a continuous function $f(x)$ over an interval from $x = a$ to $x = b$ is determined by calculating $\frac{f(b) - f(a)}{b - a}$. This is also the slope, m_S, of the secant line, l, through points $(a, f(a))$ and $(b, f(b))$.

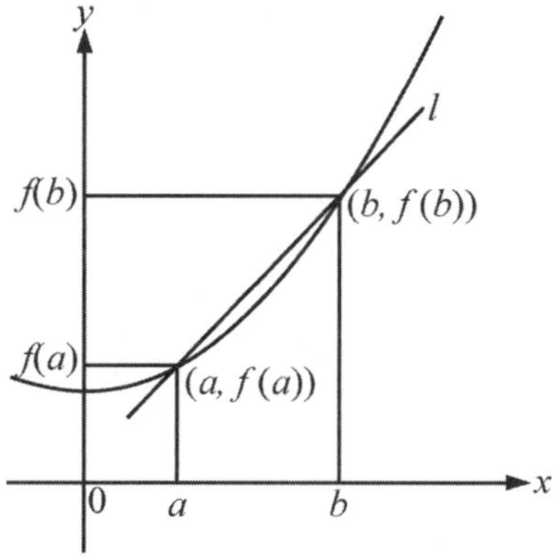

Therefore, the average rate of change over an interval from $x = a$ to $x = b$ is $m_S = \frac{f(b) - f(a)}{b - a}$.

The slope of the secant line gets closer to the slope of the tangent line at point $(a, f(a))$ as point $(b, f(b))$ moves closer to point $(a, f(a))$. Therefore, the **instantaneous rate of change** of the function at the point $(a, f(a))$ is the slope of the tangent line, m_T, at $(a, f(a))$. This can also be described as the instantaneous rate of change of y (or $f(x)$) with respect to x when $x = a$.

This diagram shows the tangent line at $(a, f(a))$.

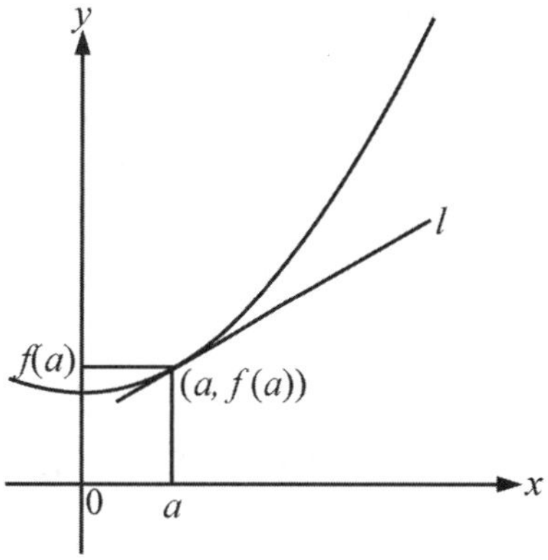

Use the following information to answer the next question.

The graph of a function, f, is given.

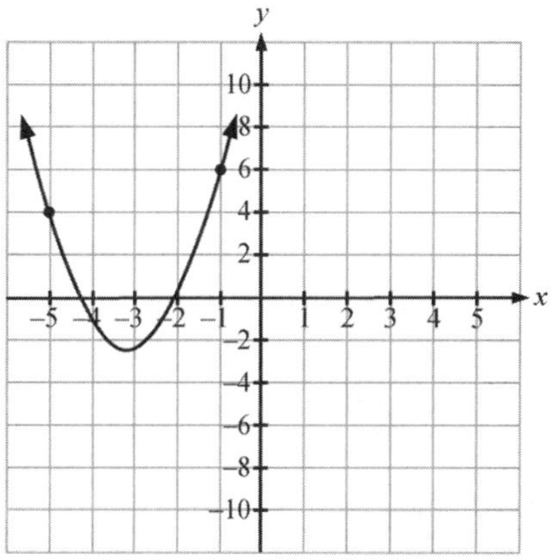

3. What is the average rate of change of f between the points $(-1, f(-1))$ and $(-5, f(-5))$?

A. -2

B. $-\frac{1}{2}$

C. $\frac{1}{2}$

D. 2

Written Response

4. For a smooth function $y = f(x)$, what does the quotient $\frac{f(x_2) - f(x_1)}{x_2 - x_1}$ represent?

RC1.3 make connections, with or without graphing technology, between an approximate value of the instantaneous rate of change at a given point on the graph of a smooth function and average rates of change over intervals containing the point (i.e., by using secants through the given point on a smooth curve to approach the tangent at that point, and determining the slopes of the approaching secants to approximate the slope of the tangent)

Approximating Instantaneous Rates of Change

The instantaneous rate of change or slope of a tangent at a fixed point of a graph of a function can be approximated by calculating the slopes of secants as one point approaches the fixed point.

The TABLE feature on a TI-83 Plus graphing calculator can be used to find the instantaneous rate of change of a given function at a particular x-value.

Example

Using the TABLE feature of a TI-83 Plus calculator and x-values of -1.1, -0.9, -1.01, -0.99, -1.001, and -0.999, estimate the instantaneous rate of change of y with respect to x for $y = x^2 - 3x$ at $x = -1$ by finding the slopes of secant lines of the corresponding graph.

Solution

Before solving the problem, set up your calculator by clearing the table entries. Press [2nd] [0], scroll down to ClrTable, and press [ENTER] twice.

Step 1
Determine the y-coordinate when $x = -1$.

$y = (-1)^2 - 3(-1)$
$y = 4$

Therefore, the stationary point for the secant lines is $(-1, 4)$.

Step 2
Enter the equations into the calculator.

Press [Y=], and enter $Y_1 = X\text{^}2 - 3X$.

To enter $Y_2 = (Y_1 - 4)/(X - (-1))$, place the cursor into $Y_2 =$. Press [(] and then [VARS]. Scroll right to access the Y-Vars Menu. Select 1:Function…, and press [ENTER] twice to bring up Y_1. Then, enter the rest of the equation.

Step 3
Generate a table for analysis.

Press [2nd] [WINDOW]. Highlight Indpnt: ASK, Depend: AUTO.

Press [2nd] [GRAPH].

Type the six x-values, -1.1, -0.9, -1.01, -0.99, -1.001, and -0.999 into the first column, pressing [ENTER] after each one. You should see the window shown here.

X	Y1	Y2
-1.1	4.51	-5.1
-.9	3.51	-4.9
-1.01	4.0501	-5.01
-.99	3.9501	-4.99
-1.001	4.005	-5.001
-.999	3.995	-4.999

X=

Step 4
Analyze the table.

The second function will give the slopes of the secant lines for the various x-values of the second point.

From the slopes of the secant lines (Y_2 in the table), you can see that the slope of the tangent line at $x = -1$ is approximately -5. Therefore, the instantaneous rate of change of y with respect to x at $x = -1$ can be estimated to be -5.

Use the following information to answer the next question.

The instantaneous rate of change of a function at $x = -3$ is 5.5.

5. Which of the following pairs of points on the graph of the function could be used to **best** approximate the instantaneous rate of change of the function at $x = -3$?

A. $(-4, -16)$ and $(-2, -4)$

B. $(-3.5, -11.31)$ and $(-3, -8)$

C. $(-3, -8)$ and $(-2.5, -5.657)$

D. $(-3.5, -11.31)$ and $(-2.5, -5.657)$

Numerical Response

6. The instantaneous rate of change of the function $y = 2x^3 - 5$ at $x = 2$, to the nearest whole number, is __________.

RC1.4 recognize, through investigation with or without technology, graphical and numerical examples of limits, and explain the reasoning involved

Understanding Limits

A **limit** is a boundary that can be approached, possibly met, and usually not exceeded.
This boundary may be a number or a line or curve that can be defined by a relation. Some functions approach asymptotes when the independent variable approaches positive or negative infinity or a value for which the function is not defined. Functions can also approach a numerical value rather than an asymptote when a variable approaches an undefined value.

For example, consider the function $y = \dfrac{3x^2+2}{x^2-1}$.

For very large values of $|x|$, the function approaches 3. This can be determined by changing the form of the function by dividing the numerator and denominator by x^2. The result is $y = \dfrac{3+\dfrac{2}{x^2}}{1-\dfrac{1}{x^2}}$.

In this form, you can see that as $x \to \pm\infty$, $\dfrac{2}{x^2}$ and $\dfrac{1}{x^2}$ approach 0. Therefore, $\dfrac{3+\dfrac{2}{x^2}}{1-\dfrac{1}{x^2}}$ approaches $\dfrac{3}{1} = 3$.

This means that

$$\lim_{x\to\infty}\frac{3x^2+2}{x^2-1} = 3 \text{ and } \lim_{x\to-\infty}\frac{3x^2+2}{x^2-1} = 3$$

Also, because the denominator of $\dfrac{3x^2+2}{x^2-1}$ cannot equal 0, $x \neq \pm 1$. As $x \to \pm 1$, the expression $\dfrac{3x^2+2}{x^2-1}$ approaches 5 divided by a number getting closer to 0, giving a result of $+\infty$.

Therefore,

$$\lim_{x\to 1}\frac{3x^2+2}{x^2-1} = \infty \text{ and } \lim_{x\to -1}\frac{3x^2+2}{x^2-1} = \infty$$

These limit results are consistent with the details of the graph of $y = \dfrac{3x^2+2}{x^2-1} = \infty$ and the graphs of its asymptotes $y = 3$, $x = 1$, and $x = -1$. These graphs, drawn using a computer graphing program, are shown here.

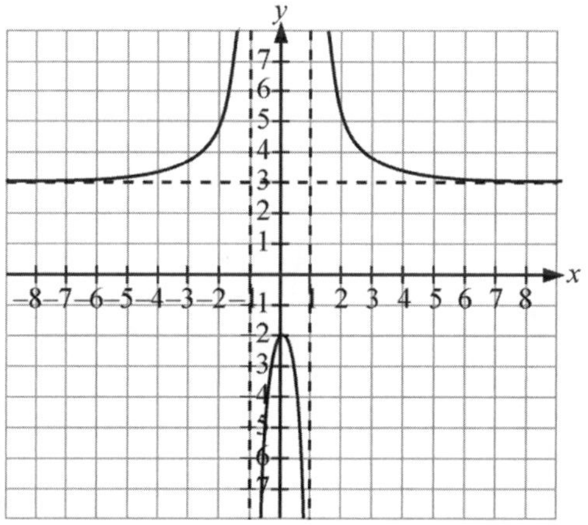

Use the following information to answer the next question.

The given table of values shows the values of a function over the interval $-5 \leq x \leq 5$, $x \in I$.

x	$f(x)$
–5	–32
–4	–16
–3	–8
–2	–4
–1	–2
0	–1
1	–0.5
2	–0.25
3	–0.125
4	–0.0625
5	–0.031 25

7. The data in the table suggests that the function has

A. at least one x-intercept

B. a hole in the graph at $x = 0$

C. a vertical asymptote at $x = 0$

D. a horizontal asymptote at $y = 0$

RC1.5 make connections, for a function that is smooth over the interval a [lesser than or equal to symbol] x [lesser than or equal to symbol] a + h, between the average rate of change of the function over this interval and the value of the expression f(a + h) – f(a)/h , and between the instantaneous rate of change of the function at x = a and the value of the limit lim[h arrow 0] f(a + h) – f(a)/h

Rates of Change and Limits

The average rate of change, or slope of the secant line, of the graph of a smooth function, $f(x)$, over the interval of $(a,\ f(a))$ to $(b,\ f(b))$ is $\frac{f(b)-f(a)}{b-a}$. If $b - a$ is designated as h, $b = a + h$, and the slope of the secant line can be written as $\frac{f(a+h)-f(a)}{h}$. A graphical representation using this notation is given.

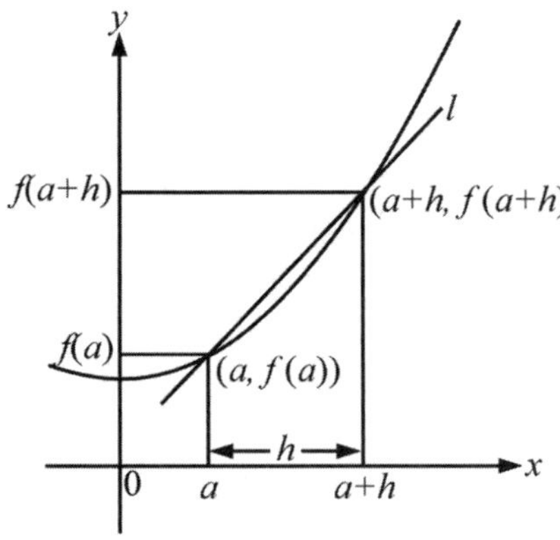

As $h \to 0$, the point $(a+h,\ f(a+h))$ approaches the point $(a,\ f(a))$, and the secant line l approaches a tangent line at $(a,\ f(a))$. The slope of this tangent line at $(a,\ f(a))$ is the instantaneous rate of change of the function at $x = a$.

Thus, the instantaneous rate of change of the function $y = f(x)$ at $x = a$ is $\lim_{h \to 0} \frac{f(a+h) - f(a)}{h}$.

Written Response

8. Discuss the difference between the meaning of $\frac{f(a+h) - f(a)}{h}$ and $\lim_{h \to 0} \frac{f(a+h) - f(a)}{h}$ for a smooth, continuous function, *f*. Provide at least one example for which the use of each expression would be most appropriate.

Use the following information to answer the next question.

> The expression $\lim_{h \to 0} \frac{\frac{2}{(-4+h)^2} - \frac{2}{(-4)^2}}{h}$ can be used to determine the instantaneous rate of change for a particular function.

Written Response

9. Determine the function $f(x)$ at the point where $x = -4$.

RC1.6 compare, through investigation, the calculation of instantaneous rates of change at a point (a, f(a)) for polynomial functions, with and without f(a + h) – f(a)/h simplifying the expression before substituting values of that approach zero

Calculating the Instantaneous Rate of Change

The instantaneous rate of change of a function, $f(x)$, at a point, $(a, f(a))$, can be predicted by using values of h that approach 0, and the expression $\frac{f(a+h) - f(a)}{h}$.

There are two methods using the expression, $\frac{f(a+h) - f(a)}{h}$, where the instantaneous rate of change can be predicted:

1. Substitute values of h that approach 0 (0.01, 0.001, 0.0001...etc) into the expression and then evaluate the expression.
2. Simplify the expression, then substitute the values of h that approach 0 (0.01, 0.001, 0.0001...etc) into the new expression.

As the value of h gets closer and closer to 0, both the simplified and non-simplified forms of the expression $\frac{f(a+h) - f(a)}{h}$ will approach a value which will be the instantaneous rate of change of a function, $f(x)$, at a point, $(a, f(a))$.

10. For which of the following functions is the instantaneous rate of change at $x = -7$ the **greatest**?

A. $f(x) = x^3$

B. $f(x) = x^3 - x$

C. $f(x) = x^2 + 9$

D. $f(x) = 2x^2 + 3x$

Written Response

11. Simplify the expression $\frac{f(a+h)-f(a)}{h}$ for the function $f(x)=x^3-1$, where $a=-5$.

RC2.1 determine numerically and graphically the intervals over which the instantaneous rate of change is positive, negative, or zero for a function that is smooth over these intervals (e.g., by using graphing technology to examine the table of values and the slopes of tangents for a function whose equation is given; by examining a given graph), and describe the behaviour of the instantaneous rate of change at and between local maxima and minima

Analyzing the Instantaneous Rate of Change with Respect to the Minima and Maxima

The instantaneous rate of change of a function can be determined from a graph or table by looking at the slopes of the tangent lines. The instantaneous rate of change of a function is:

- Positive where the slope of the tangent line is positive. This is where the graph of the function is increasing when viewed from left to right.
- Negative where the slope of the tangent line is negative. This is where the graph of the function is decreasing when viewed from left to right.
- Zero where the slope of the tangent line is zero. These points where the slope of the tangent line is zero are called *stationary points*.

The *local maxima* of a function $f(x)$ are function values where the graph achieves maximum values relative to those regions of the graph. The slopes of the tangent lines change from positive to negative at points on the graphs where the local maximums occur.

The *local minima* of a function $f(x)$ are function values where the graph achieves minimum values relative to those regions of the graph. The slopes of the tangent lines change from negative to positive at points on the graphs where the local minimums occur.

Use the following information to answer the next question.

The slope of the tangent for a smooth function is positive for $x<-3$ and $x>1$ and is negative for $-3<x<1$.

12. What is the maximum number of minima possible for the function?

A. 0 **B.** 1

C. 2 **D.** 3

Use the following information to answer the next question.

A function, f, has the following characteristics:

i. The instantaneous rate of change of f is 0 at $x=-5$, $x=-1$, and $x=4$.
ii. The rate of change of f is positive on $x<-5$ and $x>4$.
iii. The rate of change of f is negative on $-5<x<-1$ and $-1<x<4$.

Written Response

13. Sketch the graph of f.

Use the following information to answer the next question.

The graph of a smooth function is given.

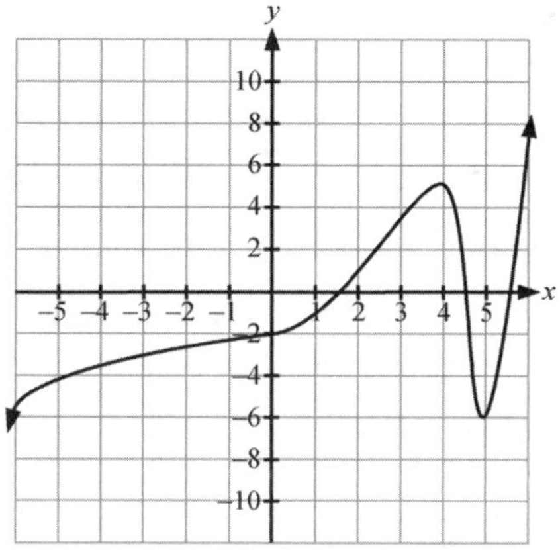

Written Response

14. On what interval is the rate of change the **greatest** for the smooth function? Justify your answer.

RC2.2 generate, through investigation using technology, a table of values showing the instantaneous rate of change of a polynomial function, f(x), for various values of x (e.g., construct a tangent to the function, measure its slope, and create a slider or animation to move the point of tangency), graph the ordered pairs, recognize that the graph represents a function called the derivative, f′(x) or dy/dx, and make connections between the graphs of f(x) and f′(x) or y and dy/dx [e.g., when f(x) is linear, f′(x) is constant; when f(x) is quadratic, f′(x) is linear; when f(x) is cubic, f′(x) is quadratic]

Analyzing the Derivatives of Polynomial Functions Graphically

The derivative of a function for any value of its variable is the instantaneous rate of change of the function for that value of the variable. For the graph of a function, the instantaneous rate of change for any value of the variable is the slope of the tangent line at the point where that value occurs.

Given a function $f(x)$, the derivative function is commonly written in one of two ways:

1. Using prime notation—$f'(x)$ is the derivative of $f(x)$. If the function is written in the $y =$ form, the derivative can be abbreviated to y'.
2. Using delta notation—$\frac{dy}{dx}$ is the instantaneous rate of change of y with respect to the x-variable.

The derivative of a function $y = f(x)$ is

$$f'(x) = \frac{dy}{dx} = \lim_{h \to 0} \frac{f(x+h) - f(x)}{h}.$$

For polynomial functions of degree n, the derivative functions are of degree $n - 1$. Therefore, when $f(x)$ is linear, $f'(x)$ is constant; when $f(x)$ is quadratic, $f'(x)$ is linear; when $f(x)$ is cubic, $f'(x)$ is quadratic, and so on.

The following features can be determined when comparing the graphs of $f(x)$ and $f'(x)$:

- $f(x)$ has a local maximum or minimum when $f'(x)$ is equal to 0.
- Wherever $f'(x)$ is positive (above the x-axis), $f(x)$ increases.
- Wherever $f'(x)$ is negative (below the x-axis), $f(x)$ decreases.

Use the following information to answer the next question.

The graph of a polynomial function $y = f(x)$ is given.

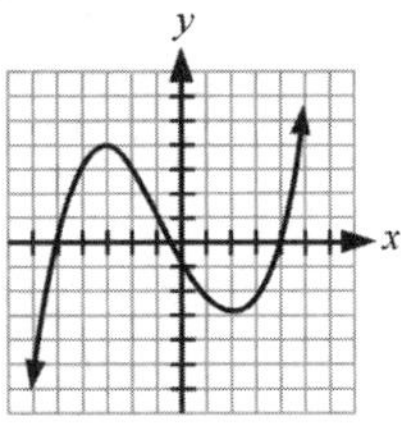

15. Which of the following graphs represents the graph of the derivative of the polynomial function $y = f(x)$?

A.

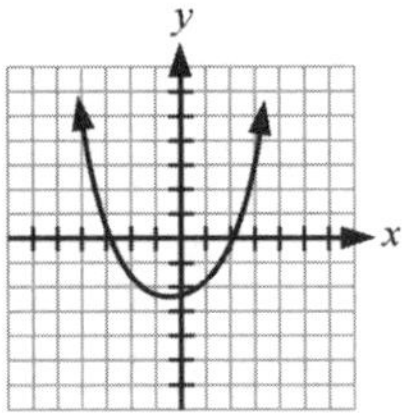

B.

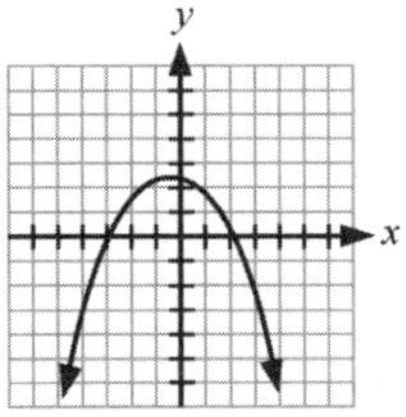

C.

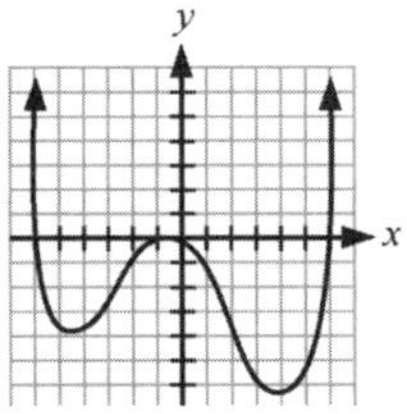

D.

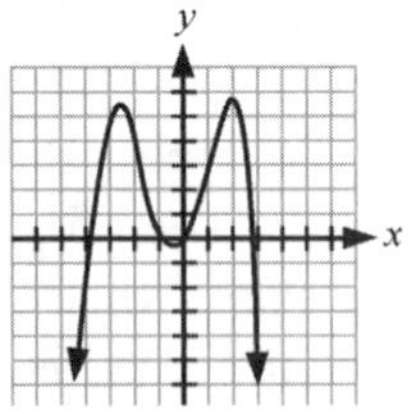

RC2.3 determine the derivatives of polynomial functions by simplifying the algebraic expression f(x + h) – f(x)/h and then taking the limit of the simplified expression as h approaches zero [i.e., determining lim[h arrow 0] f(x + h) – f(x)/h]

Determining the Derivative of a Polynomial Function Using the Definition of the Derivative

The derivative of a specific polynomial function can be determined algebraically using the definition of the derivative, $f'(x) = \frac{dy}{dx}$

$= \lim_{h \to 0} \frac{f(x+h) - f(x)}{h}$.

Use the following steps to take the derivative of a polynomial using the definition of a derivative:

1. Expand and simplify the expressions $f(x+h)$ and $f(x)$.
2. Substitute the equations for $f(x)$ and $f(x+h)$ into the equation $\lim_{h \to 0} \frac{f(x+h) - f(x)}{h}$, and simplify.
3. Factor h out of all the terms in the numerator.
4. Divide out the common factor, h, and determine the limit by substituting 0 for h.

16. Which of the following expressions can be used to determine the value of $f'(0)$ for $f(x) = -12x + 9$ from the definition of the derivative?

A. $\lim_{h \to 0} \frac{-12(h+9) - 9}{h}$

B. $\lim_{h \to 0} \frac{(-12h+9) - 9}{h}$

C. $\lim_{h \to 0} \frac{(-12+9)(h+0) - 9}{h}$

D. $\lim_{h \to 0} \frac{-12(h+9) - (-12+9)}{h}$

Written Response

17. When using the definition of the derivative, $f'(x) = \lim_{h \to 0} \frac{f(x+h) - f(x)}{h}$, to determine $f'(x)$ for $f(x) = x^2 + 5x - 11$, identify the simplified expression in the numerator of the limit just before substituting 0 for h.

RC2.4 determine, through investigation using technology, the graph of the derivative f'(x)or dy of a given sinusoidal function [i.e., dx f(x) = sin x, f(x) = cos x] (e.g., by generating a table of values showing the instantaneous rate of change of the function for various values of x and graphing the ordered pairs; by using dynamic geometry software to verify graphically that when f(x) = sin x, f'(x) = cos x, and when f(x) = cos x, f'(x) = –sin x; by using a motion sensor to compare the displacement and velocity of a pendulum)

The Derivatives of Sinusoidal Functions

The functions $f(x) = \sin x$ and $f(x) = \cos x$ are both sinusoidal functions, each with a period of 2π. It follows that the derivatives of these functions will also be sinusoidal, each with a period of 2π. As with other functions, the graphs of sinusoidal functions and their derivatives can be investigated by using a table of values or graphing technology in which the following can be determined.

- If $f(x) = \sin x$, then $f'(x) = \cos x$.
- If $f(x) = \cos x$, then $f'(x) = -\sin x$.

18. Which of the following calculator screen shots (each using the window $x:\left[-2\pi, 2\pi, \frac{\pi}{4}\right] y:[-2, 2, 1]$) corresponds to the graph of the derivative of the sinusoidal function $f(x) = -\sin x$?

A.

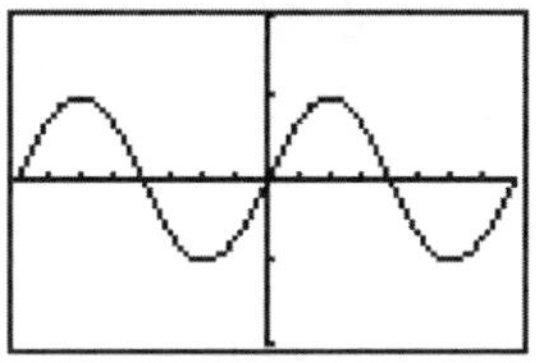

B.

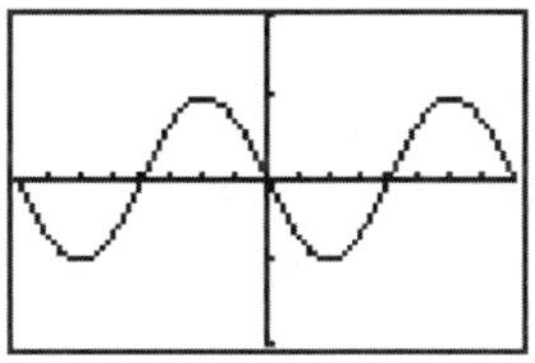

C.

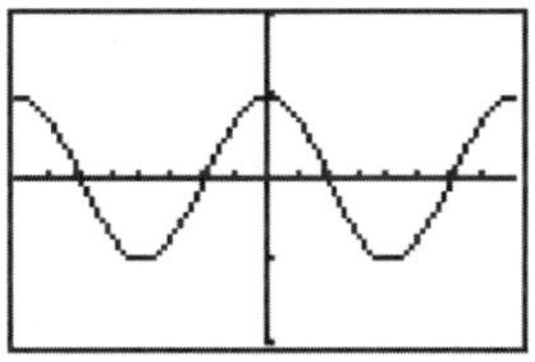

D.

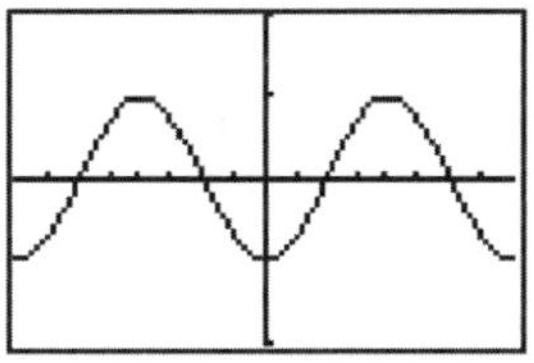

RC2.5 determine, through investigation using technology, the graph of the derivative f'(x)or dy/dx of a given exponential function [i.e., f(x) = a(x) (a > 0, a ≠ 1)], and make connections between the graphs of f(x) and f'(x) or y and dy/dx

ANALYZING THE DERIVATIVES OF EXPONENTIAL FUNCTIONS GRAPHICALLY

An exponential function is a function of the form $f(x) = a^x$, where $a > 0$ and $a \neq 1$.

The graphs for $f(x) = \left(\frac{1}{2}\right)^x$ and $f(x) = 2^x$, from a TI-83 graphing calculator, are shown.

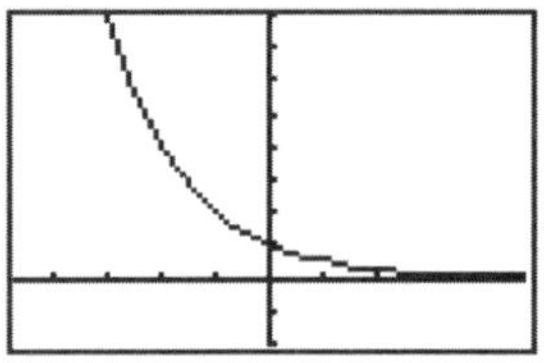

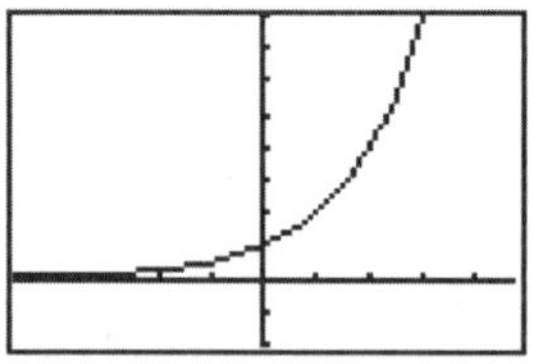

When $0 < a < 1$, from left to right the graph falls toward the x-axis, and the derivative of the function will always be negative since it is always decreasing. When $a > 1$, from left to right the graph rises from near the x-axis, and the derivative of the function will always be positive since it is always increasing.

The derivative of an exponential function is related to the function itself by $f'(x) = kf(x)$, where k is a constant, and the value of k varies with the value of a.

19. Given the function $f(x) = 5^{3x}$, the ratio $\frac{f'(x)}{f(x)}$, to the nearest thousandth, is

A. 0.207 **B.** 0.536

C. 1.864 **D.** 4.828

Written Response

20. Using technology, generate a table of values that shows the instantaneous rate of change of the function $f(x) = \left(\frac{1}{4}\right)^x$ on the interval $-4 \leq x \leq 4$, $x \in I$.

RC2.6 determine, through investigation using technology, the exponential function f(x) = a(x) (a > 0, a ≠ 1) for which f'(x) = f(x) (e.g., by using graphing technology to create a slider that varies the value of a in order to determine the exponential function whose graph is the same as the graph of its derivative), identify the number e to be the value of a for which f'(x) = f(x) [i.e., given f(x) = e(x), f (x) = e(x)], and recognize that for the exponential function f(x) = e(x) the slope of the tangent at any point on the function is equal to the value of the function at that point

ANALYZING THE DERIVATIVES OF EXPONENTIAL FUNCTIONS WHEN $f'(x) = f(x)$

For functions of the form $f(x) = a^x$, the derivative function is of the form $f'(x) = kf(x)$, where k is a constant. Also, the value of k varies with the value of a.

One approach to finding a value of a for the function $f(x) = a^x (a > 0,\ a \neq 1)$ so that $f'(x) = f(x)$ (the value of k is 1) is to plot the graphs of $y = f(x) = a^x$ and its derivative $y = f'(x)$ for various values of a until the graphs appear to overlap.

After enough trials, the graphs will overlap at a number known as Euler's number, *e*.
The number *e* is an irrational number. When written as a decimal, it neither terminates nor repeats. The first 13 decimal places are $2.718\,281\,8284\,(59)$.
The derivative of $f(x) = e^x$ is $f'(x) = e^x$. It is the only function whose derivative is the function itself.
This means that the instantaneous rate of change of $f(x) = e^x$ at any value of x is e^x, which is also the slope of the tangent line of the graph at that particular x-value.

Use the following information to answer the next question.

The slope of the tangent for the function $f(x) = a^x$ is 1 at the point (0, 1).

Numerical Response

21. Calculated to the nearest hundredth, the value of a is ________.

RC2.7 recognize that the natural logarithmic function f(x) = log(e)x, also written as f(x) = ln x, is the inverse of the exponential function f(x) = e(x), and make connections between f(x) = ln x and f(x) = e(x)

Investigating the Natural Logarithmic Function $f(x) = \ln x$

A **natural logarithm** is any logarithm with a base of the unique numeric value *e*. The value of *e* is unique because the function of $f(x) = e^x$ has the derivative of $f'(x) = e^x$. The inverse of $f(x) = e^x$ is the natural logarithmic function, $f(x) = \log_e x$. The notation ln, pronounced "lawn," is used to represent the natural logarithm $\log_e$. Therefore, the function $f(x) = \log_e x$ is written as $f(x) = \ln x$. The graphs of $y = e^x$ and $y = \ln x$ will appear as reflections across the line $y = x$ since two inverse relations are graphed as reflections in the line $y = x$.

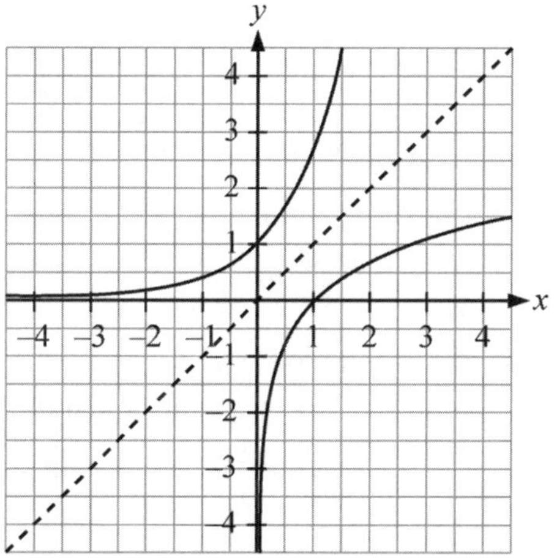

The functions of $y = e^x$ and $y = \ln x$

Since $f(x) = e^x$ and $f(x) = \ln x$ are inverse functions, the operation of one undoes the operation of the other. Consider the composite function $g(x) = e^{\ln x}$. Let $x = 20$ therefore $g(20) = e^{\ln 20}$. The value of ln 20 is approximately 3.0, and the value of $e^{\approx 3.0}$ is 20. Therefore, $g(20) = e^{\ln 20} = 20$.

Generally, $e^{\ln x} = x$ and $\ln e^x = x$.

22. What is the value of x in the equation $e^{4-x} = 12$?

A. $x = e^{-8}$

B. $x = -8$

C. $x = \ln(12) - 4$

D. $x = 4 - \ln(12)$

RC2.8 verify, using technology (e.g., calculator, graphing technology), that the derivative of the exponential function f(x) = a(x) is f′(x) = ax ln a for various values of a

Investigating the Derivative of Exponential Functions Algebraically

Given an exponential function of the form $f(x) = a^x$, the derivative is related to the function itself by $f'(x) = kf(x)$, where k is a constant, and the value of k varies with the value of a. By building a table of values and comparing the value of $a^x \ln(a)$ to the expression, $\frac{f(x+h)-f(x)}{h}$, where x is any value and h is a value that is approaching 0, it can be verified that the value of k is equal to $\ln a$. Therefore, if $f(x) = a^x$, then the derivative of the function is $f'(x) = a^x \ln(a)$.

23. The value of $f'(1.5)$ for the function $f(x) = 4^x$, to the nearest hundredth, is

A. 0.41 **B.** 1.39

C. 8.50 **D.** 11.09

RC3.1 verify the power rule for functions of the form f(x) = x(n), where n is a natural number

The Power Rule on Functions of the Form $f(x) = x^n$, Where n is a Natural Number

The derivative of a polynomial function of degree n is of degree $n - 1$. The derivatives of polynomial functions of the form $f(x) = x^n$, where n is a natural number, have a specific form that is described by the power rule.

The power rule states that the derivative of $f(x) = x^n$, where $n \in N$, is $f'(x) = nx^{n-1}$.

24. The derivative of $y = t^{k+1}$, $k \in \mathbb{N}$, gives a result of

A. $\frac{dy}{dt} = (k+1)t^k$

B. $\frac{dy}{dt} = (k-1)t^k$

C. $\frac{dy}{dt} = kt^{k-1}$

D. $\frac{dy}{dt} = kt^k$

RC3.2 verify the constant, constant multiple, sum, and difference rules graphically and numerically, and read and interpret proofs involving lim[h arrow 0] f(x + h) – f(x)/h of the constant, constant multiple, sum, and difference rules (student reproduction of the development of the general case is not required)

The Constant, Constant Multiple, Sum, and Difference Rules

When taking the derivative of a function, the following rules should be considered:

- The constant rule—the derivative of $f(x) = k$, where $k \in \mathbb{R}$, is $f'(x) = 0$.
- The constant multiple rule—the derivative of $g(x) = kf(x)$, where $k \in \mathbb{R}$, is $g'(x) = kf'(x)$.
- The sum rule—$f'(x) + g'(x) = (f+g)'(x)$.
- The difference rule—$f'(x) - g'(x) = (f-g)'(x)$.

Recognizing and interpreting proofs of the derivative rules can be done using the definition of the derivative, $\lim_{h \to 0} \frac{f(x+h)-f(x)}{h}$.

25. Which rule is illustrated by the statement that the derivative of $f(x) = 7$ is $f'(x) = 0$?

A. Sum rule

B. Constant rule

C. Difference rule

D. Constant multiple rule

Written Response

26. Explain and illustrate how the difference rule for derivatives could be verified graphically and numerically for the functions $f(x) = 3x^2$ and $g(x) = x^3$.

RC3.3 determine algebraically the derivatives of polynomial functions, and use these derivatives to determine the instantaneous rate of change at a point and to determine point(s) at which a given rate of change occurs

Using Derivatives of Polynomials to Determine an Instantaneous Rate of Change Algebraically

The power, constant, constant multiple, sum, and difference rules can be applied to finding the derivatives of many polynomial functions. Once the derivative of a polynomial function, $f(x)$, is determined, it can be used to do the following:

- The instantaneous rate of change of a function, $f(x)$, at a point can be determined by substituting the value of the x-coordinate into the derivative and solving for $f'(x)$.
- The point or points where a function, $f(x)$, changes at a particular rate can be determined by substituting the rate of change for $f'(x)$ in the derivative and solving for x.

27. The instantaneous rate of change of the function $f(x) = x^4 - 11x^2 + 7x - 1$ at $x = 0$ is

A. $f'(0) = -1$

B. $f'(0) = 0$

C. $f'(0) = 2$

D. $f'(0) = 7$

28. For the function $f(x) = -3x^5 + 12x^2 - 15$, $f'(2)$ is equal to

A. -63 **B.** -129

C. -192 **D.** -288

Numerical Response

29. Given the function $f(x) = x^2 - 3$, the y-coordinate of the highest point on the graphs of $f(x)$ and $f'(x)$ that satisfies the equation $f(x) = f'(x)$ is __________.

Written Response

30. Find the x-coordinates of the points on the curve of $f(x) = x^3 - x^2 - x + 1$ where the tangent line to $f(x)$ is horizontal.

RC3.4 verify that the power rule applies to functions of the form f(x) = x(n), where n is a rational number, and verify algebraically the chain rule using monomial functions and the product rule using polynomial functions

The Power, Chain, and Product Rules

The power, chain, and product rules can be applied to determine the derivatives of various functions. Each rule can be verified by comparing the derivatives of functions that were determined by using different methods.

The Power Rule

The power rule states that the derivative of $f(x) = x^n$ is $f'(x) = nx^{n-1}$. It applies when n is a rational number (a number of the form $\frac{A}{B}$, where A and B are integers and $B \neq 0$). To verify the power rule, the values of the slopes of tangents to a function $f(x)$ can be compared to the values of its derivative function $f'(x)$ found using the power rule.

The Chain Rule

For functions that are of the form $f(x) = g(h(x))$, the derivative is often found by using the chain rule. The derivative of $f(x) = g(h(x))$ is $f'(x) = g'(h(x))h'(x)$.

Applying the chain rule to a function of the form $f(x) = (h(x))^n$ gives a derivative of $f'(x) = n(h(x))^{n-1}h'(x)$. If the function $h(x)$ is a monomial, the chain rule can be verified by finding the same derivative from a simplified form of $(h(x))^n$.

The Product Rule

Derivatives of functions of the form $f(x) = g(x)h(x)$ are often found by using the product rule. The derivative of $f(x) = g(x)h(x)$ is $f'(x) = g(x)h'(x) + g'(x)h(x)$.

The product rule can be abbreviated as $(gh)' = gh' + g'h$.

If a function is a product of other functions, the product rule can be verified by finding the derivative of a simplified form of the product.

31. Which of the following functions could be used to verify the product rule for finding the derivative of $f(x) = (3x^2 - 3)(5x^3 + 2x)$?

A. $f(x) = 75x^4 - 6$

B. $f(x) = 15x^5 - 6x$

C. $f(x) = 15x^5 - 9x^3 - 6x$

D. $f(x) = 75x^4 - 27x^2 - 6$

*RC3.5 solve problems, using the product and chain rules, involving the derivatives of polynomial functions, sinusoidal functions, exponential functions, rational functions, radical functions, and other simple combinations of functions**

Applying the Product and Chain Rules

The product and chain rules can be used to determine the derivatives of a variety of polynomial and non-polynomial functions. To apply the chain rule, rewrite a function as a power function.
To apply the product rule, change the form of a function from a quotient to a product. The latter type involves the application of both rules.

Example

Determine $\frac{dy}{dx}$ if $y = \sqrt{x^2 - 4x}$.

Solution

Step 1
Change the radical to a power.

$$\begin{aligned} y &= \sqrt{x^2 - 4x} \\ &= (x^2 - 4x)^{\frac{1}{2}} \end{aligned}$$

Step 2
Apply the chain rule.

$$\begin{aligned} y &= (x^2 - 4x)^{\frac{1}{2}} \\ \frac{dy}{dx} &= \frac{1}{2}(x^2 - 4x)^{-\frac{1}{2}}\left(\frac{d}{dx}(x^2 - 4x)\right) \\ &= \frac{1}{2}(x^2 - 4x)^{-\frac{1}{2}}(2x - 4) \\ &= \frac{2x - 4}{2(x^2 - 4x)^{\frac{1}{2}}} \\ &= \frac{x - 2}{(x^2 - 4x)^{\frac{1}{2}}} \\ &= \frac{x - 2}{\sqrt{x^2 - 4x}} \end{aligned}$$

Example

Determine the derivative of $f(x) = \frac{x-2}{x^2+2}$.

Solution

Step 1

Change the function from quotient form to product form.

$$f(x) = \frac{x-2}{x^2+2} = (x-2)(x^2+2)^{-1}$$

Step 2

Let $g(x) = x - 2$ and $h(x) = (x^2+2)^{-1}$, and determine $g'(x)$ and $h'(x)$.

$$g(x) = x - 2$$
$$g'(x) = 1$$
$$h(x) = (x^2+2)^{-1}$$
$$h'(x) = -2x(x^2+2)^{-2}$$

Step 3

Apply the product rule to determine $f'(x)$.

$$f(x) = g(x)h(x)$$
$$f'(x) = g'(x)h(x) + g(x)h'(x)$$
$$= \left(\begin{array}{l} (x^2+2)^{-1} \\ + (x-2)(-2x(x^2+2)^{-2}) \end{array} \right)$$
$$= \frac{1}{x^2+2} - \frac{2x(x-2)}{(x^2+2)^2}$$

---

32. The derivative $\frac{dy}{dx}$ of $y = -3x^3e^{2x}$ is

A. $-18x^2e^{2x}$

B. $-3x^3e^{2x} - 9x^2e^{2x}$

C. $-6x^3e^{2x} - 9x^2e^{2x}$

D. $-3x^3e^2 - 9x^2e^{2x}$

Numerical Response

33. To the nearest tenth, what is the value of $f'(1)$ given $f(x) = \frac{(7x-3)^2}{3x^3}$? ________

Written Response

34. Determine the equation of the tangent line to the curve defined by $y = (1+x^3)^{\frac{3}{2}}$ at the point (2, 27).

Written Response

35. Determine the derivative of $y = \frac{e^{3x}}{x^3}$.

Use the following information to answer the next question.

The functions t and u are differentiable at $x = 3$.

Written Response

36. If $t(3) = 4$, $t'(3) = 5$, $u(3) = -2$, and $u'(3) = -1$, determine the value of the derivative of tu when $x = 3$.

Answers and Solutions

Rate of Change

1. B	9. WR	17. WR	25. B	33. 2.7
2. B	10. A	18. D	26. WR	34. WR
3. C	11. WR	19. D	27. D	35. WR
4. WR	12. B	20. WR	28. C	36. WR
5. D	13. WR	21. 2.72	29. 6	
6. 24	14. WR	22. D	30. WR	
7. D	15. A	23. D	31. C	
8. WR	16. B	24. A	32. C	

1. B

A positive rate of change means that as an independent variable increases, the dependent variable increases. Consider each of the given variables individually.

The temperature of water being heated over time increases as the time of heating increases.

The tension of a spring increases as the amount of compression increases.

The average monthly temperature in Canada increases from January to May (as the months of the year increase).

The fuel economy of a vehicle decreases as a vehicle increases its speed. This does not represent a positive rate of change because as the independent variable (speed) increases, the dependent variable (fuel economy) decreases.

2. B

Step 1
Determine the position, s, at $t = 0$.

$$\begin{aligned} s &= 2t - 5 \\ &= 2(0) - 5 \\ &= -5 \text{ m} \end{aligned}$$

Step 2
Determine the position, s, at $t = 5$.

$$\begin{aligned} s &= 2t - 5 \\ &= 2(5) - 5 \\ &= 5 \text{ m} \end{aligned}$$

Step 3
Determine the rate of change of the object.

Since the object moves from –5 m to 5 m (a total of 10 m) in 5 s, the rate of change is $\frac{10 \text{ m}}{5 \text{ s}} = 2.0$ m/s.

3. C

The average rate of change is the slope, m, between the points $(-1, 6)$ and $(-5, 4)$.

$$\begin{aligned} m &= \frac{4-6}{-5-(-1)} \\ &= \frac{-2}{-4} \\ &= \frac{1}{2} \end{aligned}$$

Therefore, the average rate of change is $\frac{1}{2}$ units of y for every unit of x.

4. WR

The quotient $\frac{f(x_2) - f(x_1)}{x_2 - x_1}$ represents the slope of the secant line through the points $(x_2, f(x_2))$ and $(x_1, f(x_1))$. It also represents the average rate of change of the function $y = f(x)$ over the interval from x_1 to x_2.

5. D

To best approximate the instantaneous rate of change of the function at $x = -3$, choose points close to $x = -3$ on both sides of the point.

The closest pair of points (excluding the point at $x = -3$) among the given pairs of points is $(-3.5, -11.31)$ and $(-2.5, -5.657)$.

6. 24

Use technology or a table of values to determine the instantaneous rate of change at $x = 2$ by finding the slopes of secant lines passing through the point $x = 2$ and points with x-values close by, such as $x = 1.99$, $x = 2.01$, $x = 1.999$, and $x = 2.001$.

Note that the point at $x = 2$ is $(2,\ 2(2)^3 - 5) = (2,\ 11)$.

Value of x	Point	Slope of Secant
1.99	(1.99, 10.7612)	$\frac{10.7612 - 11}{1.99 - 2}$ $= 23.88$
2.01	(2.01, 11.2412)	$\frac{11.2412 - 11}{2.01 - 2}$ $= 24.12$
1.999	(1.999, 10.9760)	$\frac{10.9760 - 11}{1.999 - 2}$ $= 24$
2.001	(2.001, 11.024)	$\frac{11.024 - 11}{2.001 - 2}$ $= 24$

According to the table of values, the slope of the secant line approaches a value of 24. Therefore, the instantaneous rate of change at $x = 2$ is 24.

7. D

The table of values shows that there is no vertical asymptote or hole at $x = 0$, since the point $(0, -1)$ exists. As x approaches larger positive values, $f(x)$ approaches 0, which implies a horizontal asymptote at $y = 0$ and no x-intercept.

8. WR

The expression $\frac{f(a+h) - f(a)}{h}$ can be used for calculating average rates of change; for example, the average speed of a vehicle between $t = a$ and $t = a + h$. The expression $\lim_{h \to 0} \frac{f(a+h) - f(a)}{h}$ can be used for calculating instantaneous rates of change; for example, the instantaneous speed of a vehicle at $t = a$.

9. WR

The instantaneous rate of change at $x = a$ for a function, f, can be determined using the expression $\lim_{h \to 0} \frac{f(a+h) - f(a)}{h}$.

In the expression $\lim_{h \to 0} \frac{\frac{2}{(-4+h)^2} - \frac{2}{(-4)^2}}{h}$,

$f(a) = \frac{2}{(-4)^2}$, when $a = -4$. Therefore, when $x = a$, the function is $f(x) = \frac{2}{x^2}$.

10. A

For each function, calculate the expression $\lim_{h \to 0} \frac{f(x+h) - f(x)}{h}$ for $x = -7$.

Step 1

$f(x) = x^3$

$$\lim_{h \to 0} \frac{(-7+h)^3 - (-7)^3}{h}$$
$$= \lim_{h \to 0} \frac{(49 - 14h + h^2)(-7+h) - (-343)}{h}$$
$$= \lim_{h \to 0} \frac{(-343 + 147h - 21h^2 + h^3) + 343}{h}$$
$$= \lim_{h \to 0} \frac{147h - 21h^2 + h^3}{h}$$
$$= \lim_{h \to 0} \frac{h(147 - 21h + h^2)}{h}$$
$$= 147$$

Step 2

$f(x) = x^3 - x$

$$\lim_{h \to 0} \frac{((-7+h)^3 - (-7+h)) - ((-7)^3 - (-7))}{h}$$
$$= \lim_{h \to 0} \frac{(-343 + 147h - 21h^2 + h^3 + 7 - h) - (-343 + 7)}{h}$$
$$= \lim_{h \to 0} \frac{146h - 21h^2 + h^3}{h}$$
$$= \lim_{h \to 0} \frac{h(146 - 21h + h^2)}{h}$$
$$= 146$$

Step 3

$f(x) = x^2 + 9$

$$\lim_{h \to 0} \frac{((-7+h)^2 + 9) - ((-7)^2 + 9)}{h}$$
$$= \lim_{h \to 0} \frac{(49 - 14h + h^2 + 9) - (49 + 9)}{h}$$
$$= \lim_{h \to 0} \frac{-14h + h^2}{h}$$
$$= \lim_{h \to 0} \frac{h(-14 + h)}{h}$$
$$= -14$$

Step 4

$f(x) = 2x^2 + 3x$

$$\lim_{h \to 0} \frac{(2(-7+h)^2 + 3(-7+h)) - (2(-7)^2 + 3(-7))}{h}$$
$$= \lim_{h \to 0} \frac{(2(49 - 14h + h^2) - 21 + 3h) - (98 - 21)}{h}$$
$$= \lim_{h \to 0} \frac{(98 - 28h + 2h^2 - 21 + 3h) - (77)}{h}$$
$$= \lim_{h \to 0} \frac{-25h + 2h^2}{h}$$
$$= \lim_{h \to 0} \frac{h(-25 + 2h)}{h}$$
$$= -25$$

11. WR

Simplify $\frac{f(a+h) - f(a)}{h}$ for $f(x) = x^3 - 1$, where $a = -5$.

$$\frac{f(a+h) - f(a)}{h}$$
$$= \frac{f(-5+h) - f(-5)}{h}$$
$$= \frac{((-5+h)^3 - 1) - ((-5)^3 - 1)}{h}$$
$$= \frac{((-5+h)(25 - 10 + h^2) - 1) - (-125 - 1)}{h}$$
$$= \frac{(-125 + 75h - 15h^2 + h^3 - 1) - (-126)}{h}$$
$$= \frac{75h - 15h^2 + h^3}{h}$$
$$= \frac{h(75 - 15h + h^2)}{h}$$
$$= 75 - 15h + h^2$$
$$= h^2 - 15h + 75$$

12. B

For the function to have slopes of tangents that are positive for $x < -3$ and negative for $-3 < x < 1$, there must be a local maximum at $x = -3$.

For the slopes of tangents to go from negative for $-3 < x < 1$ to positive for $x > 1$, there must be a local minimum at $x = 1$. Therefore, the maximum number of minima is 1.

13. WR

There is a local maximum at $x = -5$ because the instantaneous rate of change is equal to 0 at $x = -5$ while the rate of change is positive on the interval $x < -5$ and negative on the interval $-5 < x < -1$. Similarly, there is a local minimum at $x = 4$ because the instantaneous rate of change is equal to 0 at $x = 4$ while the rate of change is negative on $-1 < x < 4$ and positive on $x > 4$. There is also a turning point at $x = -1$ since the slope of the graph is 0 at $x = -1$ while being negative on $-5 < x < -1$ and $-1 < x < 4$.

The graph drawn should resemble the one shown here.

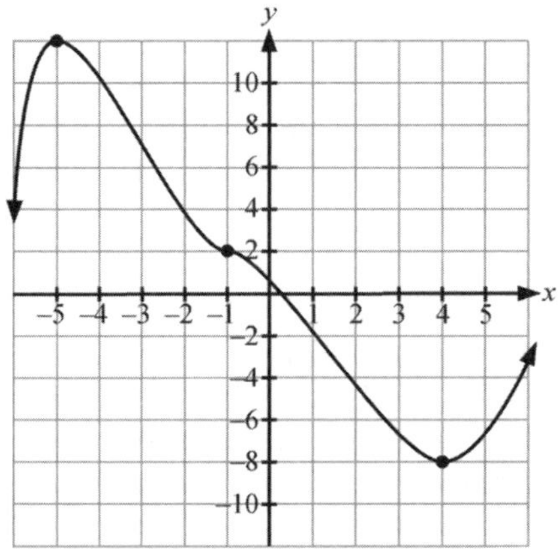

14. WR

The rate of change is greatest for $x > 5$ because the slopes of the tangents on this interval are the greatest. The slopes are positive and very large because the graph is steepest on this interval.

15. A

At approximately $x = -3$ and $x = 2$, the slopes of the tangents of $y = f(x)$ are 0. Therefore, the graph of the derivative is equal to zero at $x = -3$ and $x = 2$. The slopes of the tangents of $y = f(x)$ in the intervals $x < -3$ and $x > 2$ are positive, and the slopes of the tangents in the interval $-3 < x < 2$ are negative. Therefore, the graph of the derivative is positive in the intervals $x < -3$ and $x > 2$ and negative in the interval $-3 < x < 2$.

This graph fits these descriptions, so it is the graph of the derivative of the function $y = f(x)$.

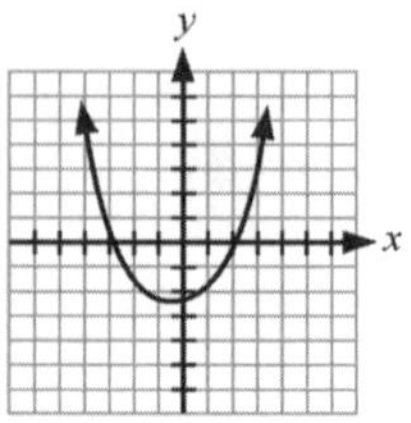

Also, since the original polynomial function looks cubic, the derivative function should look quadratic.

16. B

The derivative of a function, $f(x)$, is $f'(x) = \lim_{h \to 0} \frac{f(x+h) - f(x)}{h}$.

To determine $f'(0)$, substitute $x = 0$ and simplify the limit for $f(x) = -12x + 9$.

$$\begin{aligned} f'(0) &= \lim_{h \to 0} \frac{f(0+h) - f(0)}{h} \\ &= \lim_{h \to 0} \frac{(-12(0+h)+9) - (-12(0)+9)}{h} \\ &= \lim_{h \to 0} \frac{(-12h+9) - (9)}{h} \end{aligned}$$

The simplified expression for $f'(0)$ is $\lim_{h \to 0} \frac{(-12h+9) - 9}{h}$.

17. WR

Simplify the definition of the derivative for $f(x) = x^2 + 5x - 11$.

$$\begin{aligned} &f'(x) \\ &= \lim_{h \to 0} \frac{f(x+h) - f(x)}{h} \\ &= \lim_{h \to 0} \frac{\left((x+h)^2 + 5(x+h) - 11\right) - \left(x^2 + 5x - 11\right)}{h} \\ &= \lim_{h \to 0} \frac{x^2 + 2xh + h^2 + 5x + 5h - 11 - x^2 - 5x + 11}{h} \\ &= \lim_{h \to 0} \frac{2xh + h^2 + 5h}{h} \\ &= \lim_{h \to 0} \frac{h(2x + h + 5)}{h} \\ &= \lim_{h \to 0} 2x + h + h \end{aligned}$$

The simplified expression in the numerator of the limit is $2x + h + 5$.

18. D

The derivative of $f(x) = \sin(x)$ is $f'(x) = \cos(x)$. Therefore, the derivative of $f(x) = -\sin(x)$ is $f'(x) = -\cos(x)$.

Verify using a graphing calculator by entering in the function and its derivative, $Y_1 = -\sin(X)$ and $Y_2 = \text{nDeriv}(Y_1, X, X)$, as y-values and pressing [GRAPH].

The following screen shot corresponds to the graph of the derivative of the sinusoidal function $f(x) = -\sin x$:

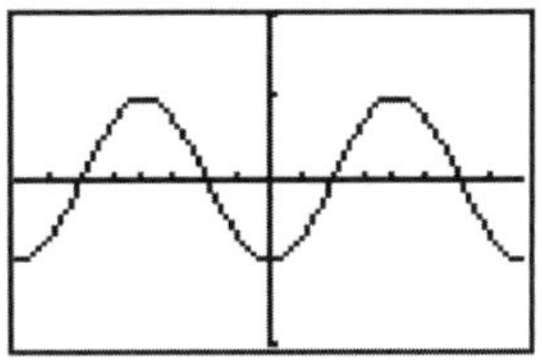

19. D

On a graphing calculator, enter the function, its derivative, and the quotient $\frac{f'(x)}{f(x)}$ as y-values.

$Y_1 = 5\text{^}(3X)$
$Y_2 = \text{nDeriv}(Y_1, X, X)$
$Y_3 = Y_2/Y_1$

Adjust the window settings to x:[−2, 2, 1] and y:[−1, 8, 1]. Press [GRAPH], and use the trace function to determine the ratio $\frac{f'(x)}{f(x)}$.

$$\begin{aligned} Y_3 &= \frac{Y_2}{Y_1} \\ &\approx 4.828 \end{aligned}$$

20. WR

Step 1
Clear all entries in the table of a TI-83 or similar calculator.

Press [2nd] [0], scroll down to ClrTable, and press [ENTER] twice.

Step 2
Enter the given function into the [Y =] editor of the calculator.

Press [Y =], enter $\left(\frac{1}{4}\right)^x$ in Y_1, and press [ENTER].

Step 3
Enter the derivative of the given function in Y_2.

Press [MATH], and select 8:nDeriv(. Press [VARS], and scroll right to select Y-VARS. Select 1:Function… and then 1:Y_1. Press [,] to insert a comma, and then enter X, X).

Step 4
Create a table that shows x, $f(x)$, and the instantaneous rate of change of the function on the interval $-4 \leq x \leq 4, x \in I$.

Press 2nd WINDOW to bring up the TBLSET menu. Enter –4 in TblStart= and 1 in ΔTbl=. Then, press 2nd GRAPH. Scroll down to see all the values in the given table.

x	$f(x)$	Rate of Change
–4	256	– 354.9
–3	64	–88.72
–2	16	–22.18
–1	4	–5.545
0	1	–1.386
1	0.25	–0.3466
2	0.0625	–0.0866
3	0.015 63	–0.0217
4	0.003 91	–0.0054

21. 2.72

The slope of the tangent at any point for $f(x) = e^x$ is equal to the value of the function at that point, since the derivative of $f(x) = e^x$ is $f'(x) = e^x$. It is the only function whose derivative is the function itself. Therefore, if the slope at $(0, 1)$ is 1, the function must be $f(x) = e^x$, where $e \approx 2.72$ to the nearest hundredth.

22. D

Step 1
Take the natural logarithm of both sides of the equation.

$$e^{4-x} = 12$$
$$\ln\left(e^{4-x}\right) = \ln(12)$$

Step 2
Simplify the equation.

Since $\ln\left(e^x\right) = x$, then $\ln\left(e^{4-x}\right) = 4 - x$. Substitute $4 - x$ for $\ln\left(e^{4-x}\right)$ in the equation and isolate x.

$$\ln\left(e^{4-x}\right) = \ln(12)$$
$$4 - x = \ln(12)$$
$$x = 4 - \ln(12)$$

23. D

The derivative of $f(x) = a^x$ is $f'(x) = a^x \ln(a)$. Therefore, $f'(1.5)$ for the function $f(x) = 4^x$ can be calculated as follows:

$$f(x) = 4^x$$
$$f'(x) = 4^x \ln(4)$$
$$f'(1.5) = 4^{1.5} \ln(4)$$
$$f'(1.5) \approx 8(1.386\ 294\ 361)$$
$$f'(1.5) \approx 11.09$$

24. A

The power rule states that the derivative of $f(x) = x^n, n \in \mathbb{N}$, is $f'(x) = nx^{n-1}$. Therefore, applying the power rule will give the following result:

$$y = t^{k+1}$$
$$\frac{dy}{dx} = (k+1)t^{(k+1)-1}$$
$$\frac{dy}{dx} = (k+1)t^k$$

25. B

The constant rule states that the derivative of $f(x) = k$, where $k \in \mathbb{R}$, is $f'(x) = 0$.

The function $f(x) = 7$ has a k-value of 7, which is a value in the real number domain, and has a derivative of $f'(x) = 0$.

Therefore, the constant rule is being illustrated by the statement that the derivative of $f(x) = 7$ is $f'(x) = 0$.

26. WR

Graphically, verification would show that the graphs of $f'(x) - g'(x)$ and $(f - g)'(x)$ are identical. Numerically, verification could come in the form of a table of values in which $f'(x) - g'(x)$ is shown to be equal to $(f - g)'(x)$ for the chosen values of x.

Verified graphically:

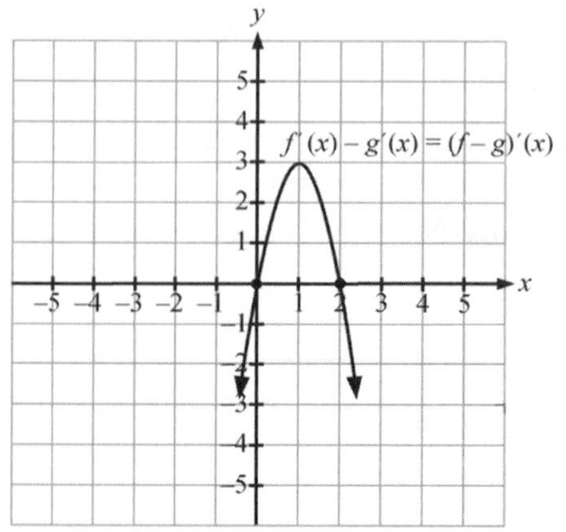

Verified numerically:
Some possible values for verification are shown in the given table.

x	$f'(x) = 6x$	$g'(x) = 3x^2$	$f'(x) - g'(x) = 6x - 3x^2$	$(f - g)'(x) = 6x - 3x^2$
–3	–18	27	–45	–45
–2	–12	12	–24	–24
–1	–6	3	–9	–9
0	0	0	0	0
1	6	3	3	3
2	12	12	0	0
3	18	27	–9	–9

27. D

Step 1
Apply the power rule to determine the derivative of the function $f(x) = x^4 - 11x^2 + 7x - 1$.

$$f(x) = x^4 - 11x^2 + 7x - 1$$
$$f'(x) = 4x^3 - 22x + 7$$

Step 2
Substitute 0 for x in the equation $f'(x) = 4x^3 - 22x + 7$, and solve for $f'(0)$ to determine the instantaneous rate of change at $x = 0$.

$$f'(x) = 4x^3 - 22x + 7$$
$$\begin{aligned} f'(0) &= 4(0)^3 - 22(0) + 7 \\ &= 7 \end{aligned}$$

28. C

Step 1
Apply the power rule to determine the derivative of $f(x) = -3x^5 + 12x^2 - 15$.

$$f(x) = -3x^5 + 12x^2 - 15$$
$$f'(x) = -15x^4 + 24x$$

Step 2
Substitute 2 for x in the equation $f'(x) = -15x^4 + 24x$, and solve for $f'(2)$.

$$f'(x) = -15x^4 + 24x$$
$$\begin{aligned} f'(2) &= -15(2)^4 + 24(2) \\ &= -240 + 48 \\ &= -192 \end{aligned}$$

29. 6

Step 1
Apply the power rule to determine the derivative of the function $f(x) = x^2 - 3$.

$$f(x) = x^2 - 3$$
$$f'(x) = 2x$$

Step 2
Equate $f(x)$ with $f'(x)$, and solve for x.

$$\begin{aligned} f(x) &= f'(x) \\ x^2 - 3 &= 2x \\ x^2 - 2x - 3 &= 0 \\ (x - 3)(x + 1) &= 0 \end{aligned}$$

Therefore, $x = 3$ and $x = -1$.

Step 3
Substitute $x = 3$ into the equation $f(x) = x^2 - 3$, and solve for $f(3)$.

$$f(x) = x^2 - 3$$
$$\begin{aligned} f(3) &= (3)^2 - 3 \\ &= 9 - 3 \\ &= 6 \end{aligned}$$

Step 4
Substitute $x = -1$ into the equation $f(x) = x^2 - 3$, and solve for $f(-1)$.

$$f(x) = x^2 - 3$$
$$\begin{aligned} f(-1) &= (-1)^2 - 3 \\ &= 1 - 3 \\ &= -2 \end{aligned}$$

The points (3, 6) and (–1, –2) both satisfy the equation $f(x) = f'(x)$. The y-coordinate of the highest point is $y = 6$.

30. WR

When the tangent line of $f(x)$ is horizontal, $f'(x) = 0$.

Step 1
Apply the power law to determine the derivative of the function $f(x) = x^3 - x^2 - x + 1$.

$$f(x) = x^3 - x^2 - x + 1$$
$$f'(x) = 3x^2 - 2x - 1$$

Step 2
Substitute 0 for $f'(x)$ into the equation $f'(x) = 3x^2 - 2x - 1$, and solve for x.

$$\begin{aligned} f'(x) &= 3x^2 - 2x - 1 \\ 0 &= 3x^2 - 2x - 1 \\ 0 &= 3x^2 - 3x + x - 1 \\ 0 &= 3x(x - 1) + (x - 1) \\ 0 &= (3x + 1)(x - 1) \end{aligned}$$

Therefore, $x = -\frac{1}{3}$ and $x = 1$.

31. C

Simplify the function $f(x) = (3x^2 - 3)(5x^3 + 2x)$.

$$\begin{aligned} f(x) &= (3x^2 - 3)(5x^3 + 2x) \\ &= 15x^5 + 6x^3 - 15x^3 - 6x \\ &= 15x^5 - 9x^3 - 6x \end{aligned}$$

Therefore, the function $f(x) = 15x^5 - 9x^3 - 6x$ could be used to verify the product rule.

32. C

Let $g(x) = -3x^3$ and $h(x) = e^{2x}$.

Step 1
Determine $g'(x)$ and $h'(x)$.

$$\begin{aligned} g(x) &= -3x^3 \\ g'(x) &= -9x^2 \\ h(x) &= e^{2x} \\ h'(x) &= e^{2x}\left(\frac{d}{dx}2x\right) \\ &= 2e^{2x} \end{aligned}$$

Step 2
Determine the derivative of the equation $y = -3x^3e^{2x}$ by applying the product rule.

$$\begin{aligned} y &= g(x)h(x) \\ \frac{dy}{dx} &= g'(x)h(x) + g(x)h'(x) \\ &= (-9x^2)(e^{2x}) + (-3x^3)(2e^{2x}) \\ &= -9x^2e^{2x} - 6x^3e^{2x} \\ &= -6x^3e^{2x} - 9x^2e^{2x} \end{aligned}$$

33. 2.7

Step 1
Rewrite the function in product form.

$$\begin{aligned} f(x) &= \frac{(7x-3)^2}{3x^3} \\ &= (7x-3)^2(3x^3)^{-1} \\ &= (7x-3)^2\left(\frac{1}{3}x^{-3}\right) \end{aligned}$$

Let $g(x) = (7x - 3)^2$and $h(x) = \frac{1}{3}x^{-3}$.

Step 2
Determine $g'(x)$ and $h'(x)$.

$$\begin{aligned} g(x) &= (7x-3)^2 \\ g'(x) &= 2(7x-3)\left(\frac{d}{dx}(7x-3)\right) \\ &= 2(7x-3)(7) \\ &= 98x - 42 \\ h(x) &= \frac{1}{3}x^{-3} \\ h'(x) &= -x^{-4} \end{aligned}$$

Step 3
Apply the product rule to find $f'(x)$.

$$\begin{aligned} f(x) &= g(x)h(x) \\ f'(x) &= g'(x)h(x) + g(x)h'(x) \\ &= \begin{pmatrix} (98x-42)\left(\frac{1}{3}x^{-3}\right) \\ + (7x-3)^2(-x^{-4}) \end{pmatrix} \\ &= \begin{pmatrix} 32.\overline{66}x^{-2} - 14x^{-3} \\ - 49x^{-2} + 42x^{-3} - 9x^{-4} \end{pmatrix} \\ &= -16.\overline{33}x^{-2} + 28x^{-3} - 9x^{-4} \end{aligned}$$

Step 4
Substitute 1 for x into the equation $f'(x) = -16.\overline{33}x^{-2} + 28x^{-3} - 9x^{-4}$, and solve for $f'(1)$.

$$\begin{aligned} f'(x) &= -16.\overline{33}x^{-2} + 28x^{-3} - 9x^{-4} \\ f'(1) &= -16.\overline{33}(1)^{-2} + 28(1)^{-3} - 9(1)^{-4} \\ &= -16.\overline{33} + 28 - 9 \\ &= 2.\overline{66} \\ &\approx 2.7 \end{aligned}$$

34. WR

Step 1
Apply the chain rule to determine the derivative of the equation $y = (1 + x^3)^{\frac{3}{2}}$.

$$\begin{aligned} y &= (1+x^3)^{\frac{3}{2}} \\ \frac{dy}{dx} &= \frac{3}{2}(1+x^3)^{\frac{1}{2}}\left(\frac{d}{dx}(1+x^3)\right) \\ \frac{dy}{dx} &= \frac{3}{2}(1+x^3)^{\frac{1}{2}}(3x^2) \\ \frac{dy}{dx} &= \frac{9}{2}x^2\sqrt{1+x^3} \end{aligned}$$

Step 2
Find the slope of the tangent line at (2, 27).

Solve for $\frac{dy}{dx}$ when $x = 2$.

$$\begin{aligned} \frac{dy}{dx} &= \frac{9}{2}x^2\sqrt{1+x^3} \\ &= \frac{9}{2}(2)^2\sqrt{1+(2)^3} \\ &= \frac{9}{2}(4)\sqrt{1+8} \\ &= 18\sqrt{9} \\ &= 18(3) \\ &= 54 \end{aligned}$$

Step 3
Substitute 2 for x, 27 for y, and 54 for m into the equation of a line formula $y = mx + b$, and solve for b.

$$\begin{aligned} y &= mx + b \\ 27 &= 54(2) + b \\ 27 &= 108 + b \\ -81 &= b \end{aligned}$$

The equation of the tangent line that goes through the point (2, 27) is $y = 54x - 81$.

35. WR

Step 1

Convert the equation $y = \dfrac{e^{3x}}{x^3}$ into product form.

$$\begin{aligned} y &= \frac{e^3x}{x^3} \\ &= e^{3x}\left(x^{-3}\right) \end{aligned}$$

Let $g(x) = e^{3x}$ and $h(x) = x^{-3}$.

Step 2
Determine $g'(x)$ and $h'(x)$.

$$\begin{aligned} g(x) &= e^{3x} \\ g'(x) &= 3e^{3x} \end{aligned}$$

and

$$\begin{aligned} h(x) &= x^{-3} \\ h'(x) &= -3x^{-4} \end{aligned}$$

Step 3
Apply the product law to determine the derivative of $y = \dfrac{e^3x}{x^3}$.

$$\begin{aligned} y &= g(x)h(x) \\ \frac{dy}{dx} &= g'(x)h(x) + g(x)h'(x) \\ \frac{dy}{dx} &= \left(3e^{3x}\right)\left(x^{-3}\right) + \left(e^{3x}\right)\left(-3x^{-4}\right) \\ \frac{dy}{dx} &= 3x^{-3}e^{3x} - 3x^{-4}e^{3x} \\ \frac{dy}{dx} &= 3x^{-4}e^{3x}(x - 1) \\ \frac{dy}{dx} &= \frac{3e^{3x}(x - 1)}{x^4} \end{aligned}$$

36. WR

When finding the derivative of tu, apply the product law.

$$\begin{aligned} (tu)'(x) &= t'(x)u(x) + t(x)u'(x) \\ (tu)'(3) &= t'(3)u(3) + t(3)u'(3) \\ &= (5)(-2) + (4)(-1) \\ &= -10 - 4 \\ &= -14 \end{aligned}$$

UNIT TEST — RATE OF CHANGE

1. Which of the following graphs **best** represents the flow rate of a glacier-fed river in Canada as a function of the month of the year?

A.

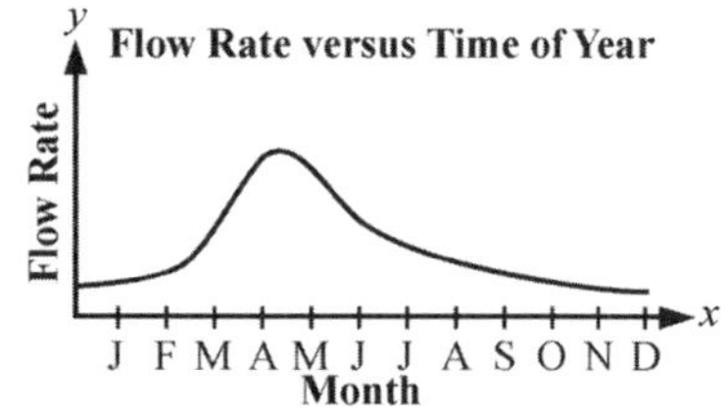

B.

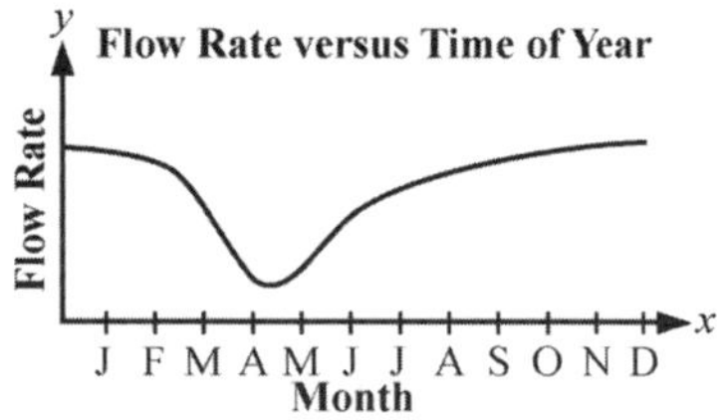

C.

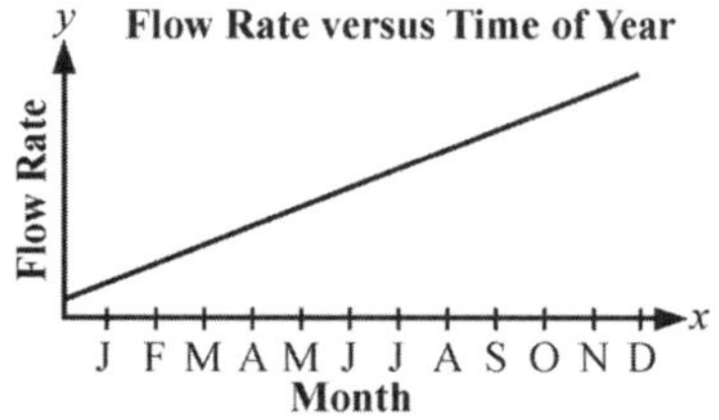

D.

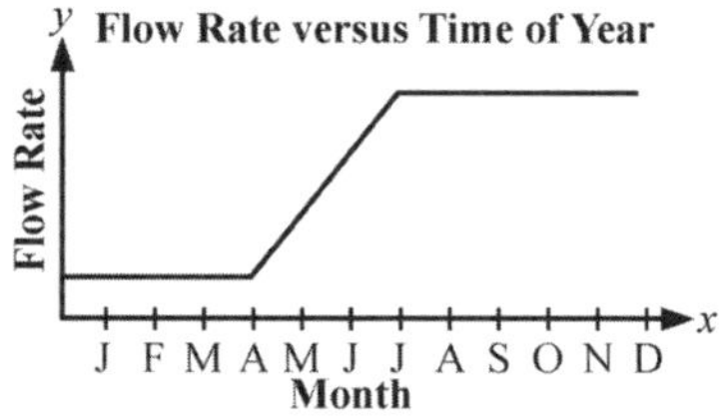

Use the following information to answer the next question.

The given table shows the rate of change of some entity with respect to time for a particular situation.

Time	1	4	8	10
Rate of change with respect to time	2	16	256	1 024

2. Which of the following situations would **most likely** create the data in the given table?

A. A farmer recording population numbers when breeding rabbits

B. A passenger recording speeds as a vehicle accelerates to highway speeds

C. A pilot recording the air temperature as an airplane descends from 37 000 ft

D. A student recording the temperature on a thermometer when it is placed in a pot of boiling water

Use the following information to answer the next question.

Newton's law of cooling states that the rate of change of the temperature of an object is proportional to the difference between its own temperature and the temperature of its surroundings.

3. A thermometer that has been stored at room temperature is placed in a bucket of ice. The absolute value of the instantaneous rate of change in the thermometer's temperature reading will be

A. constant

B. greatest immediately after being inserted in the ice

C. greatest as it approaches the temperature of the ice

D. equal to the average rate of change over a given time interval

Use the following information to answer the next question.

For five years, the front porch of a home has been sinking a little bit more each year. The given table shows the year and corresponding sinking depth of the porch.

Year	Sinking Depth (cm)
2000	1.50
2001	3.10
2002	4.80
2003	6.70
2004	8.70
2005	10.90

4. Calculated to the nearest hundredth, what was the average rate of change in the depth over this period?

A. 1.44 cm/a **B.** 1.56 cm/a

C. 1.57 cm/a **D.** 1.88 cm/a

Use the following information to answer the next question.

The position, s, in metres, of a particle at a time, t, in seconds, is given by the equation $s = 2t^2 - 3t + 3$, where $t \geq 0$.

5. Which of the following pairs of points would provide the **best** approximation of the instantaneous rate of change when the particle's position is 8 m?

A. $t = 0.4$ s and $t = 0.6$ s

B. $t = 0.9$ s and $t = 1.1$ s

C. $t = 1.4$ s and $t = 1.6$ s

D. $t = 2.4$ s and $t = 2.6$ s

Use the following information to answer the next question.

The position, s, in metres, of an object after a time, t, in seconds, is defined by the function $s = t^2 + 2t - 8$.

Numerical Response

6. Calculated to the nearest tenth, the instantaneous rate of change of the object's position with respect to time when $t = 3.5$ is __________ m/s.

Use the following information to answer the next question.

The general term of a sequence is defined by the equation $t_n = 4 + \frac{1}{2n}$.

7. As n becomes infinitely large, t_n approaches

A. 0 **B.** 4

C. 4.5 **D.** infinity

Use the following information to answer the next question.

Jamie determined that the expression $\frac{f(5+h)-f(5)}{h}$ is 0 and concluded that the average rate of change of the function between $x=5$ and $x=h$ is 0. Based on her findings, she made the following remarks: I. The slope of the secant from $x=5$ to $x=h$ is 0. II. The slope of the tangent to the function at $x=5$ is 0. III. $f(5+h)=f(5)$ IV. The function has a maximum at $x=5$.

8. Which of the given statements are certain?

A. I and II **B.** I and III

C. II and IV **D.** III and IV

Written Response

9. Provide an example of a function, f, for which the evaluation of the expression $\lim_{h \to 0} \frac{f(a+h)-f(a)}{h}$ would be unnecessary for determining the instantaneous rate of change of f at $x=a$.

Written Response

10. In simplified form, determine an expression equivalent to $\frac{f(-1+h)-f(-1)}{h}$ for the function $f(x)=3x^2-1$.

Written Response

11. What expression can be used to approximate the instantaneous rate of change of a function or to calculate the average rate of change of a function?

12. Which of the following statements about a smooth and continuous curve is **true**?

A. To the immediate left of a local minimum, the slopes of the tangents to the curve are positive.

B. To the immediate left of a local maximum, the slopes of the tangents to the curve are negative.

C. To the immediate right of a local minimum, the slopes of the tangents to the curve are positive.

D. On either immediate side of a local maximum, the slopes of the tangents to the curve are negative.

13. For which of the following values of x is the instantaneous rate of change of the function $y=x^4+3x^3+6x^2-4x-6$ equal to zero?

A. 0 only **B.** 0.25 only

C. 0 and –2 **D.** 0.25 and –2

Use the following information to answer the next question.

A table of values for a continuous function and the slopes of its tangents is given.

x	$f(x)$	**Slope of Tangent**
−10	$-87.\bar{3}$	35
−9	−58	24
−8	$-38.\bar{6}$	15
−7	$-27.\bar{3}$	8
−6	−22	3
−5	$-20.\bar{6}$	0
−4	$-21.\bar{3}$	−1
−3	−22	0
−2	$-20.\bar{6}$	3
−1	$-15.\bar{3}$	8
	−4	105

Written Response

14. Assuming the slope of the tangent is zero only at the x-values indicated in the table, and its sign changes only at these values, identify the intervals or values for which the instantaneous rates of change of the given function are positive, negative, and zero.

15. If a polynomial function is quadratic, then the derivative of the function is

A. cubic **B.** linear

C. constant **D.** quadratic

16. Using the definition of a derivative, the value of $f'(5)$ for $f(x) = -3x^2 + 4x$ is determined from

A. $\lim\limits_{h \to 0} \dfrac{-3(5+h)^2 - 4(5+h) - \left(3(5)^2 - 4(5)\right)}{h}$

B. $\lim\limits_{h \to 0} \dfrac{-3(5+h)^2 + 4(5+h) - \left(3(5)^2 + 4(5)\right)}{h}$

C. $\lim\limits_{h \to 0} \dfrac{-3(5+h)^2 + 4(5+h) - \left(-3(5)^2 + 4(5)\right)}{h}$

D. $\lim\limits_{h \to 0} \dfrac{-3(5+h)^2 + 4(5+h) - \left(-3(5)^2 - 4(5)\right)}{h}$

Written Response

17. Use the definition of the derivative to determine $\dfrac{dy}{dx}$ for $y = x^3 - 4x + 9$.

18. If the derivative of a certain function is $f'(x) = 2\sin(x)$, the function is

A. $f(x) = 2\cos(x)$

B. $f(x) = \cos(2x)$

C. $f(x) = -2\cos(x)$

D. $f(x) = -\cos(2x)$

19. Which of the following tables of values corresponds to the instantaneous rates of change, $f'(x)$, of the function $f(x) = -\cos x$?

A.

x	$f'(x)$
0	0
$\frac{\pi}{4}$	0.7071
$\frac{\pi}{2}$	1
$\frac{3\pi}{4}$	0.7071
π	0

B.

x	$f'(x)$
0	0
$\frac{\pi}{4}$	–0.7071
$\frac{\pi}{2}$	1
$\frac{3\pi}{4}$	–0.7071
π	0

C.

x	$f'(x)$
0	1
$\frac{\pi}{4}$	0.7071
$\frac{\pi}{2}$	0
$\frac{3\pi}{4}$	–0.7071
π	–1

D.

x	$f'(x)$
0	–1
$\frac{\pi}{4}$	–0.7071
$\frac{\pi}{2}$	0
$\frac{3\pi}{4}$	0.7071
π	1

20. Which of the following graphs could represent the graph of the derivative of the function $f(x) = \left(\frac{2}{5}\right)^{2x}$?

A.

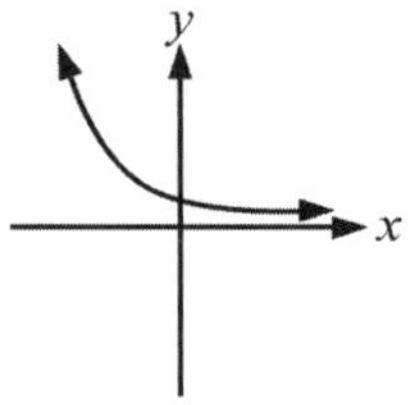

B.

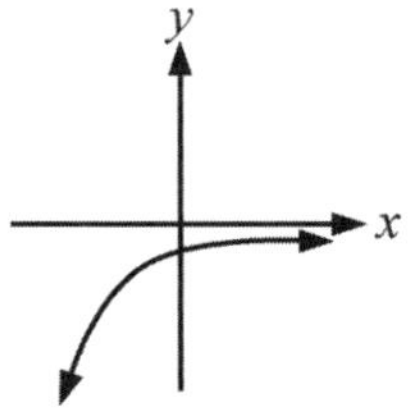

C.

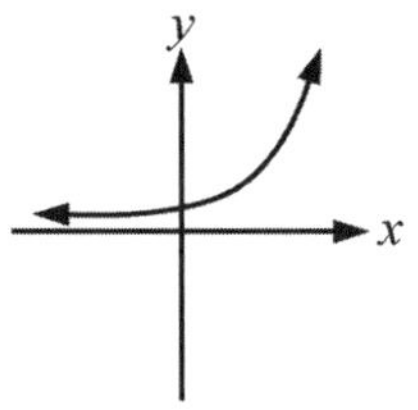

D.

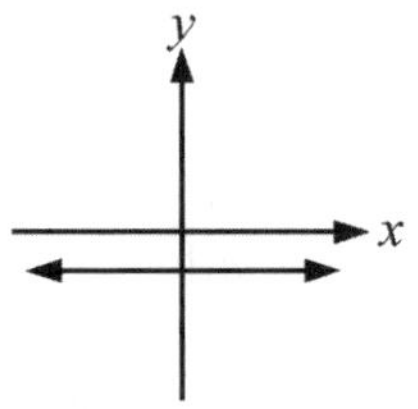

21. For which of the following types of functions could the ratio between the derivative of the function and the function itself be constant?

A. Linear
B. Sinusoidal
C. Polynomial
D. Exponential

Numerical Response

22. Given the function $f(x) = e^x$, the value of $f'(2.5)$ to the nearest tenth is ________.

Numerical Response

23. Rounded to the nearest whole number, the value of x in the equation $\ln(e^{2x-1}) = 5$ is ________.

24. To the nearest thousandth, the slope of the tangent of the function $f(x) = \left(\frac{1}{3}\right)^x$ at $x = 3$ is

A. -0.041 **B.** 0.037

C. 0.041 **D.** 1.000

25. Which of the following equations uses the definition of a derivative to verify the power rule for finding the derivative of $f(x) = x^4$?

A. $f(x) = x^4$

B. $f'(x) = 4x^3$

C. $f'(x) = \dfrac{(x+h)^4 - x^4}{h}$

D. $f'(x) = \lim\limits_{h \to 0} \dfrac{(x+h)^4 - x^4}{h}$

26. If $f(x) = 3x^3$ and $g(x) = -2f(x)$, then the graph of $g'(x)$ is the graph of $f'(x)$ after a vertical stretch by a factor of

A. 2 about the x-axis

B. $\frac{1}{2}$ about the x-axis

C. 2 about the x-axis and a reflection in the x-axis

D. $\frac{1}{2}$ about the x-axis and a reflection in the x-axis

27. Which of the following functions have the same derivative?

A. $f(x) = 3x^2$ and $f(x) = 2x^3$

B. $f(x) = 4x$ and $f(x) = x + 4$

C. $f(x) = 5x^2 - 12$ and $f(x) = 5x^2 + 7$

D. $f(x) = x^4 - 5x + 4$ and $f(x) = 2x^2 - 5x + 4$

28. At what point on the graph of the function $f(x) = x^3 + 2x^2 - 11x + 15$ does the slope of the tangent to the function equal -12?

A. $(1, 7)$

B. $(1, -4)$

C. $(-1, 27)$

D. $(-1, -12)$

Numerical Response

29. The functions $f(x) = \frac{2}{3}x^3 - \frac{7}{2}x^2 + x - 9$ and $g(x) = \frac{1}{3}x^3 - \frac{3}{2}x^2 - 3x + 5$ have identical instantaneous rates of change when the value of x, to the nearest whole number, is __________.

30. Which of the following expressions could be used to verify the product rule for finding the derivative of the function $f(x) = (2x - 1)^3$?

A. $6x^3 - 1$

B. $8x^3 - 1$

C. $8x^3 - 12x^2 + 6x$

D. $8x^3 - 12x^2 + 6x - 1$

31. If p, q, and r are non-zero differentiable functions in terms of x, then the derivative of $y = \frac{pq}{r}$ can be written as

A. $\dfrac{dy}{dx} = \dfrac{p'q'r - pqr'}{r^2}$

B. $\dfrac{dy}{dx} = \dfrac{pq'r + p'qr - pqr'}{r^2}$

C. $\dfrac{dy}{dx} = \dfrac{pqr' - pq'r - p'qr}{r^2}$

D. $\dfrac{dy}{dx} = \dfrac{p'qr + pq'r + pqr'}{r^2}$

Numerical Response

32. To the nearest hundredth, what is the value of x for which the tangent line of the function $f(x) = e^{3x-2}$ is equal to 50? ________

Numerical Response

33. Rounded to the nearest hundredth, the value of $|f'(\pi)|$ when $f(x) = \dfrac{\cos(x+\pi)}{4e^{2x^2-20}}$ is ________.

Written Response

34. If the coordinates are rounded to the nearest hundredth, at what point will the line tangent to the curve $y = 2xe^x$ be parallel to the line $y - x - 1 = 0$?

Written Response

35. Determine the derivative of the function $y = \sin(\sin x)$.

Written Response

36. Sketch the graphs of $f'(x) + g'(x)$ and $(f+g)'(x)$ given $f(x) = \frac{1}{3}x^3$ and $g(x) = -4x$.

Written Response

37. At what point on the graph of $f(x) = x^2 - 3$ is the line tangent to $f(x)$ perpendicular to the line $2y - x + 1 = 0$?

ANSWERS AND SOLUTIONS — UNIT TEST

1. A	9. WR	17. WR	25. D	33. 4.08
2. A	10. WR	18. C	26. C	34. WR
3. B	11. WR	19. A	27. C	35. WR
4. D	12. C	20. B	28. C	36. WR
5. D	13. B	21. D	29. 2	37. WR
6. 9.0	14. WR	22. 12.2	30. D	
7. B	15. B	23. 3	31. B	
8. B	16. C	24. A	32. 1.60	

1. A

The flow rate from January to March is very low, since most of the glacier is frozen. The flow rate from March to June increases rapidly as the warming temperatures melt the glacier. From June to September, the flow rate gradually decreases as the volume of the glacier decreases. Finally, from September to December, the flow rate is very low as the glacier becomes frozen.

2. A

The population of rabbits breeding over time is the only given situation that increases exponentially. This would mean that the rate of change increases rapidly, as illustrated in the given table.

3. B

The absolute value of the instantaneous rate of change in the thermometer's temperature just after insertion is very large since the difference between its temperature and the surrounding temperature of the ice is large. The absolute value of the instantaneous rate of change becomes less and less as the thermometer's temperature approaches the temperature of the ice.

4. D

The average rate of change over the five-year period is the slope, m, between the two points (0, 1.50) and (5, 10.90).

$$m = \frac{10.90 - 1.50}{5 - 0}$$
$$= \frac{9.40}{5}$$
$$= 1.88$$

The average rate of change in the depth is 1.88 cm/a.

5. D

Step 1

Determine the value(s) of t when the particle's position is 8 m.

$$s = 2t^2 - 3t + 3$$
$$8 = 2t^2 - 3t + 3$$
$$0 = 2t^2 - 3t - 5$$
$$t = \frac{-(-3) \pm \sqrt{(-3)^2 - 4(2)(-5)}}{2(2)}$$
$$t = \frac{3 \pm \sqrt{49}}{4}$$
$$t = \frac{3 \pm 7}{4}$$
$$t = -1 \text{ or } 2.5$$

The time when the particle's position is 8 m is 2.5 s since $t = -1$ is extraneous ($t \geq 0$).

Step 2

Determine the pair of points that will best approximate the instantaneous rate of change at $t = 2.5$ s.

Of the given alternatives, $t = 2.4$ s and $t = 2.6$ s are the best points for approximating the instantaneous rate of change at $t = 2.5$ s because they are closest to $t = 2.5$ s and are located on either side of this point.

6. 9.0

Use technology or a table of values to determine the instantaneous rate of change at $t = 3.5$ by finding the slopes of secant lines that pass through the point at $t = 3.5$ and points with t-values close by, such as $t = 3.49$, 3.51, 3.499, and 3.501. Note that the point at $t = 3.5$ is $\left(3.5,\ (3.5)^2 + 2(3.5) - 8\right) = (3.5,\ 11.25)$.

The solution can be calculated by following the steps below with a TI-83 graphing calculator or a similar calculator.

Step 1

Clear the table entries. Press [2nd] [0], scroll down to ClrTable, and press [ENTER] twice.

Step 2
Press $\boxed{\text{Y=}}$, and enter $Y_1 = X^2 + 2X - 8$.

Step 3
Enter a second function that will give the slopes of the secant lines for the various *t*-values of the second point.
The equation that will be entered is $Y_2 = (Y_1 - 11.25)/(X - 3.5)$. To enter this equation, place the cursor into $Y_2 =$. Press $\boxed{(}$ and then $\boxed{\text{VARS}}$. Scroll right to access the Y-VARS Menu. Select 1:Function…, and press $\boxed{\text{ENTER}}$ to bring up Y_1. Then, enter the rest of the equation.

Step 4
Press $\boxed{\text{2nd}}\boxed{\text{WINDOW}}$, and highlight Indpnt: ASK, Depend: AUTO.

Step 5
Press $\boxed{\text{2nd}}\boxed{\text{GRAPH}}$, and type the *t*-values 3.49, 3.51, 3.499, and 3.501 into the first column. (Press $\boxed{\text{ENTER}}$ after each entry.) You should see the screen shot shown.

X	Y1	Y2
3.49	11.16	8.99
3.51	11.34	9.01
3.499	11.241	8.999
3.501	11.259	9.001

X=

From the values in Y_2 (the slopes of secants), the instantaneous rate of change of the object's position at $t = 3.5$ s, to the nearest tenth, is 9.0 m/s.

7. B

Find the limit of t_n as n approaches infinity.

$$\lim_{n\to\infty} 4 + \frac{1}{2n}$$
$$= \lim_{n\to\infty} \frac{8n+1}{2n}$$
$$= \lim_{n\to\infty} \frac{\frac{8n}{n} + \frac{1}{n}}{\frac{2n}{n}}$$
$$= \lim_{n\to\infty} \frac{8 + \frac{1}{n}}{2}$$
$$= \frac{8+0}{2}$$
$$= 4$$

8. B

For $\frac{f(5+h)-f(5)}{h}$ to equal 0, $f(5+h) - f(5) = 0$. Therefore, $f(5+h) = f(5)$ is certain. Also, the expression $\frac{f(5+h)-f(5)}{h}$ describes the slope of the secant from $x = 5$ to $x = h$, which is 0. Statements II and IV apply to the expression $\lim_{h\to0} \frac{f(5+h)-f(5)}{h}$ and therefore are not certain. Statements I and III are certain.

9. WR

A constant function $y = c$ is a horizontal line where the instantaneous rate of change is zero for all values of x. For such a function, it would be unnecessary to evaluate the expression $\lim_{h\to0} \frac{f(a+h)-f(a)}{h}$ at $x = a$.

10. WR

Simplify $\frac{f(-1+h)-f(-1)}{h}$ for $f(x) = 3x^2 - 1$.

$$\frac{f(-1+h)-f(-1)}{h}$$
$$= \frac{(3(-1+h)^2 - 1) - (3(-1)^2 - 1)}{h}$$
$$= \frac{(3(1-2h+h^2) - 1) - (3-1)}{h}$$
$$= \frac{3 - 6h + 3h^2 - 1 - 2}{h}$$
$$= \frac{-6 + 3h^2}{h}$$
$$= \frac{h(-6+3h)}{h}$$
$$= -6 + 3h$$

11. WR

The expression $\frac{f(a+h)-f(a)}{h}$ can be used to approximate the instantaneous rate of change at $x = a$ for a function, f, or to calculate the average rate of change from $x = a + h$ to $x = a$.

12. C

At a local maximum, the slopes of the tangents to a smooth and continuous curve change from positive (to its left) to negative (to its right).

At a local minimum, the slopes of the tangents to a smooth and continuous curve change from negative (to its left) to positive (to its right).

13. B

Using a graphing calculator, graph the function using the window settings x: $[-5, 5, 1]$ and y: $[-10, 10, 1]$.

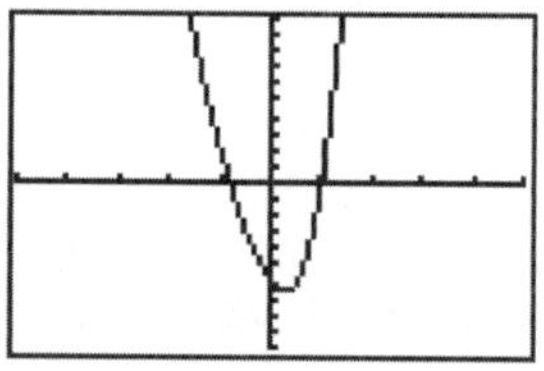

By observing the graph, it is evident that there is a minimum point at about $x = 0.25$. The slope of the tangent at this point (instantaneous rates of change) would equal zero.

14. WR

There are positive instantaneous rates of change on the intervals $-10 \leq x < -5$ and $-3 < x \leq 0$ because the slopes of tangents are all positive.

There are negative instantaneous rates of change on the interval $-5 < x < -3$ because the slopes of the tangents are all negative.

The instantaneous rates of change are zero at $x = -5$ and at $x = -3$.

15. B

The derivative of a polynomial function of degree n has a degree of $n - 1$. Therefore, the derivative of a quadratic function ($n = 2$) is linear ($n = 1$).

16. C

The derivative of a function, $f(x)$, is defined as $f'(x) = \lim\limits_{h \to 0} \frac{f(x+h) - f(x)}{h}$.

Substitute 5 into $f'(x) = \lim\limits_{h \to 0} \frac{f(x+h) - f(x)}{h}$ to determine $f'(5)$.

$$f'(5)$$
$$= \lim_{h \to 0} \frac{f(5+h) - f(5)}{h}$$
$$= \lim_{h \to 0} \frac{-3(5+h)^2 + 4(5+h) - \left(-3(5)^2 + 4(5)\right)}{h}$$

17. WR

The derivative of a function, y, is as follows:
$$\frac{dy}{dx} = \lim_{h \to 0} \frac{f(x+h) - f(x)}{h}$$

Use the definition of a derivative to solve for $\frac{dy}{dx}$ for the function $y = x^3 - 4x + 9$.

$$\frac{dy}{dx}$$
$$= \lim_{h \to 0} \frac{\left((x+h)^3 - 4(x+h) + 9\right) - \left(x^3 - 4x + 9\right)}{h}$$
$$= \lim_{h \to 0} \frac{\left((x+h)(x^2 + 2xh + h^2) - 4x - 4h + 9\right) - \left(x^3 - 4x + 9\right)}{h}$$
$$= \lim_{h \to 0} \frac{x^3 + 3xh^2 + 3x^2h + h^3 - 4x - 4h + 9 - x^3 + 4x - 9}{h}$$
$$= \lim_{h \to 0} \frac{3xh^2 + 3x^2h + h^3 - 4h}{h}$$
$$= \lim_{h \to 0} \frac{h\left(3xh + 3x^2 + h^2 - 4\right)}{h}$$
$$= \lim_{h \to 0} 3xh + 3x^2 + h^2 - 4$$
$$= 3x^2 - 4$$

18. C

The derivative of $f(x) = \cos(x)$ is $f'(x) = -\sin(x)$. Therefore, the derivative of $f(x) = -2\cos(x)$ is $f'(x) = 2\sin(x)$.

This result can also be verified by using a TI-83 or similar calculator. To do so, follow the steps below.

Step 1

Press [Y =], enter $-2\cos(x)$ in Y_1, and press [ENTER].

Step 2

Press [MATH], and select 8:nDeriv(. Press [VARS], and scroll right to select Y-VARS. Select 1:Function... and then 1:Y_1. Press [,] to insert a comma, and enter X, X). Press [ENTER].
This procedure will enter the derivative of $f(x) = -2\cos(x)$ into Y_2.

Step 3
Enter 2sin (x) in Y_3.

The three entries should appear as shown.

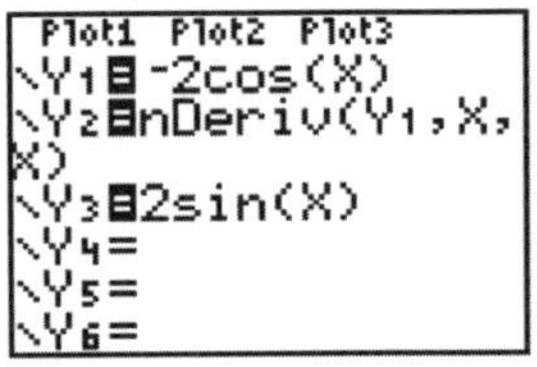

Next, press GRAPH. (Make sure that an appropriate window setting has been selected such as $x{:}\left[-\pi,\ \pi,\ \frac{\pi}{2}\right]$ and $y{:}[-3,\ 3,\ 1]$.)

Graphs Y_2 and Y_3 should be identical.

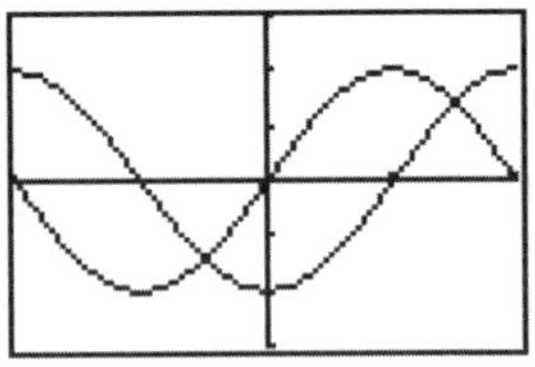

19. A

Clear all entries in the table in your calculator. Press 2nd 0 (CATALOG), then scroll to ClrTable and press ENTER twice.

Next, press Y = and enter the function $y = -\cos(x)$ and its derivative.
$Y_1 = -\cos(X)$
$Y_2 = \text{nDeriv}(Y_1, X, X)$

Then press 2nd GRAPH and enter the values $x = 0, \frac{\pi}{4}, \frac{\pi}{2}, \frac{3\pi}{4}, \pi$.

Compare the values in the table to identify the correct table.

This table corresponds to the derivative of the function $f(x) = -\cos x$.

x	$f'(x)$
0	0
$\frac{\pi}{4}$	0.7071
$\frac{\pi}{2}$	1
$\frac{3\pi}{4}$	0.7071
π	0

20. B

Press Y = on a graphing calculator, and enter the function and its derivative with a window setting of $x{:}[-1.5, 1.5, 1]$, $y{:}[-10, 10, 1]$.
$Y_1 = (2/5)\text{^}(2X)$
$Y_2 = \text{nDeriv}(Y_1, X, X)$

Press GRAPH. Notice that the graph of the derivative of $f(x)$ looks like the given graph.

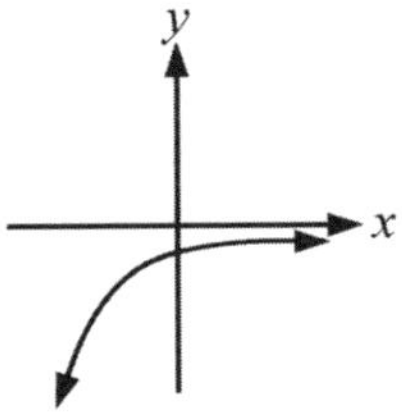

21. D

When an exponential function $f(x)$ is divided by its derivative function $f'(x)$, the quotient is $\frac{f'(x)}{f(x)} = k$, where k is a constant.

22. 12.2

The derivative of $f(x) = e^x$ is $f'(x) = e^x$.
Solve for $f'(2.5)$.
$f'(2.5) = e^{2.5}$
$= 12.182\ 493\ 96$

Rounded to the nearest tenth, $f'(2.5)$ is 12.2.

23. 3

Step 1
Since $\ln(e^x) = x$, then $\ln(e^{2x-1}) = 2x - 1$.
Substitute $2x - 1$ for $\ln(e^{2x-1})$ in the equation $\ln(e^{2x-1}) = 5$.
$\ln(e^{2x-1}) = 5$
$2x - 1 = 5$

Step 2
Solve for x.
$2x - 1 = 5$
$2x = 6$
$x = 3$

24. A

The slope of the tangent for a function $y = f(x)$ is the derivative of $f(x)$ at any value of x.
The derivative of $f(x) = a^x$ is $f'(x) = a^x \ln(a)$.

Calculate $f'(3)$ for the function $f(x)=\left(\frac{1}{3}\right)^x$.

$f'(3)$
$=\left(\frac{1}{3}\right)^x\ln\left(\frac{1}{3}\right)$
$=\left(\frac{1}{3}\right)^3\ln\left(\frac{1}{3}\right)$
$\approx(0.037\ 037\ 037)(-1.098\ 612\ 289)$
≈-0.041

25. D

According to the power rule, $f'(x)=nx^{n-1}$. Therefore, the derivative of $f(x)=x^4$ is $f'(x)=4x^3$.

The definition of a derivative is $f'(x)=\lim\limits_{h\to 0}\frac{f(x+h)-f(x)}{h}$. Calculate the derivative of $f(x)=x^4$.

$f'(x)$
$=\lim\limits_{h\to 0}\frac{(x+h)^4-x^4}{h}$
$=\lim\limits_{h\to 0}\frac{(x^4+4x^3h+6x^2h^2+4xh^3+h^4)-x^4}{h}$
$=\lim\limits_{h\to 0}\frac{4x^3h+6x^2h^2+4xh^3+h^4}{h}$
$=\lim\limits_{h\to 0}4x^3+6x^2h+4xh^2+h^3$
$=4x^3$

The result matches the result from the power rule.

Therefore, the equation $f'(x)=\lim\limits_{h\to 0}\frac{(x+h)^4-x^4}{h}$ uses the definition of a derivative to verify the power rule.

26. C

The constant multiple rule states that the derivative of $g(x)=kf(x)$, $k\in\mathbb{R}$, is $g'(x)=kf'(x)$.

If $g(x)=-2f(x)$, then $g'(x)=-2f'(x)$. Therefore, $g'(x)$ is the graph of $f'(x)$ multiplied by a factor of -2, which causes a vertical stretch by a factor of 2 about the x-axis and a reflection in the x-axis.

27. C

Step 1
Take the derivative of $f(x)=3x^2$ and $f(x)=2x^3$.
$f(x)=3x^2$
$f'(x)=6x$
$f(x)=2x^3$
$f'(x)=6x^2$
The derivatives are not the same.

Step 2
Take the derivative of $f(x)=4x$ and $f(x)=x+4$.
$f(x)=4x$
$f'(x)=4$
$f(x)=x+4$
$f'(x)=1$
The derivatives are not the same.

Step 3
Take the derivative of $f(x)=5x^2-12$ and $f(x)=5x^2+7$.
$f(x)=5x^2-12$
$f'(x)=10x$
$f(x)=5x^2+7$
$f'(x)=10x$
The derivatives are the same.

Step 4
Take the derivative of $f(x)=x^4-5x+4$ and $f(x)=2x^2-5x+4$.
$f(x)=x^4-5x+4$
$f'(x)=4x^3-5$
$f(x)=2x^2-5x+4$
$f'(x)=4x-5$
The derivatives are not the same.

28. C

Step 1
Take the derivative of the function $f(x)=x^3+2x^2-11x+15$.
$f(x)=x^3+2x^2-11x+15$
$f'(x)=3x^2+4x-11$

Step 2
Since the slope of the tangent is -12, $f'(x)=-12$. Substitute -12 for $f'(x)$ in the equation $f'(x)=3x^2+4x-11$.
$f'(x)=3x^2+4x-11$
$-12=3x^2+4x-11$
$0=3x^2+4x+1$

Step 3
Factor the equation, and solve for x.

$0 = 3x^2 + 4x + 1$
$0 = 3x^2 + 3x + x + 1$
$0 = 3x(x + 1) + (x + 1)$
$0 = (3x + 1)(x + 1)$

Therefore, the x-values are $x = -1$ and $x = -\frac{1}{3}$.

The only viable option is $x = -1$ because none of the given points have an x-value of $-\frac{1}{3}$.

Step 4
Substitute -1 for x in the function $f(x) = x^3 + 2x^2 - 11x + 15$, and solve for $f(-1)$.

$f(x) = x^3 + 2x^2 - 11x + 15$
$f(-1) = (-1)^3 + 2(-1)^2 - 11(-1) + 15$
$f(-1) = -1 + 2 + 11 + 15$
$f(-1) = 27$

Therefore, the point on the graph of $f(x) = x^3 + 2x^2 - 11x + 15$ where the slope of the tangent is -12 is $(-1, 27)$.

29. 2

Step 1
Take the derivative of the function $f(x) = \frac{2}{3}x^3 - \frac{7}{2}x^2 + x - 9$.

$f(x) = \frac{2}{3}x^3 - \frac{7}{2}x^2 + x - 9$
$f'(x) = 2x^2 - 7x + 1$

Step 2
Take the derivative of the function $g(x) = \frac{1}{3}x^3 - \frac{3}{2}x^2 - 3x + 5$.

$g(x) = \frac{1}{3}x^3 - \frac{3}{2}x^2 - 3x + 5$
$g'(x) = x^2 - 3x - 3$

Step 3
Since the instantaneous rate of change is found by taking the derivative of a function, for the two functions to have identical instantaneous rates of change, $f'(x) = g'(x)$. Equate the derivatives of the two functions, and bring all the terms to one side.

$f'(x) = g'(x)$
$2x^2 - 7x + 1 = x^2 - 3x - 3$
$x^2 - 4x + 4 = 0$

Step 4
Factor the equation, and solve for x.

$x^2 - 4x + 4 = 0$
$(x - 2)(x - 2) = 0$
$(x - 2)^2 = 0$
$x = 2$

Therefore, the functions $f(x)$ and $g(x)$ have identical instantaneous rates of change at $x = 2$.

30. D

Simplify the function $f(x) = (2x - 1)^3$.

$f(x) = (2x - 1)^3$
$= (2x - 1)(2x - 1)^2$
$= (2x - 1)(4x^2 - 4x + 1)$
$= 8x^3 - 12x^2 + 6x - 1$

The function $f(x) = 8x^3 - 12x^2 + 6x - 1$ can be used to verify the product rule for finding the derivative of the function $f(x) = (2x - 1)^3$.

31. B

Step 1

Rewrite the function $y = \frac{pq}{r}$ in product form.

$y = \frac{pq}{r}$
$= pqr^{-1}$

Step 2
Substitute f for pq, and apply the product rule to the function.

$y = pqr^{-1}$
$y = fr^{-1}$
$\frac{dy}{dx} = f'r^{-1} + f(-1r^{-2}(r'))$
$\frac{dy}{dx} = f'r^{-1} - fr'r^{-2}$

Step 3
Determine f' by applying the product rule to the function $f = pq$.

$f = pq$
$f' = pq' + p'q$

Step 4
Substitute $pq' + p'q$ for f' into the derivative $\frac{dy}{dx} = f'r^{-1} - fr'r^{-2}$, and simplify.

$\frac{dy}{dx} = f'r^{-1} - fr'r^{-2}$
$= (pq' + p'q)r^{-1} - (pq)r'r^{-2}$
$= pq'r^{-1} + p'qr^{-1} - pqr'r^{-2}$
$= \frac{pq'r + p'qr - pqr'}{r^2}$

32. 1.60

Step 1

Take the derivative of the function $f(x) = e^{3x-2}$. Apply the chain rule.

$$f(x) = e^{3x-2}$$
$$f'(x) = e^{3x-2}\left(\frac{d}{dx}(3x-2)\right)$$
$$= e^{3x-2}(3)$$
$$= 3e^{3x-2}$$

Step 2

Since $f'(x)$ is equal to the tangent line, substitute 50 for $f'(x)$ in the derivative function $f'(x) = 3e^{3x-2}$, and solve for x.

$$f'(x) = 3e^{3x-2}$$
$$50 = 3e^{3x-2}$$
$$\frac{50}{3} = e^{3x-2}$$
$$\ln\left(\frac{50}{3}\right) = \ln e^{3x-2}$$
$$\ln\left(\frac{50}{3}\right) = 3x-2$$
$$\ln\left(\frac{50}{3}\right)+2 = 3x$$
$$\frac{\ln\left(\frac{50}{3}\right)+2}{3} = x$$
$$1.604\,4702\ldots = x$$
$$1.60 \approx x$$

33. 4.08

Step 1

Change the function from quotient form to product form.

$$f(x) = \frac{\cos(x+\pi)}{4e^{2x^2-20}}$$
$$= (\cos(x+\pi))\left(\frac{1}{4}e^{-(2x^2-20)}\right)$$
$$= (\cos(x+\pi))\left(\frac{1}{4}e^{-2x^2+20}\right)$$

Step 2

Let $g(x) = \cos(x+\pi)$ and $h(x) = \frac{1}{4}e^{-2x^2+20}$.

Determine $g'(x)$ and $h'(x)$ by applying the chain rule.

$$g(x) = \cos(x+\pi)$$
$$g'(x) = -\sin(x+\pi)\left(\frac{d}{dx}(x+\pi)\right)$$
$$g'(x) = -\sin(x+\pi)(1)$$
$$g'(x) = -\sin(x+\pi)$$
$$h(x) = \frac{1}{4}e^{-2x^2+20}$$
$$h'(x) = \frac{1}{4}e^{-2x^2+20}\left(\frac{d}{dx}(-2x^2+20)\right)$$
$$h'(x) = \frac{1}{4}e^{-2x^2+20}(-4x)$$
$$h'(x) = -xe^{-2x^2+20}$$

Step 3

Determine the derivative of $f(x)$ by applying the product rule.

$$f(x) = g(x)h(x)$$
$$f'(x) = g'(x)h(x) + g(x)h'(x)$$
$$f'(x) = \begin{pmatrix} (-\sin(x+\pi))\left(\frac{1}{4}e^{-2x^2+20}\right) \\ + \ (\cos(x+\pi))\left(-xe^{-2x^2+20}\right) \end{pmatrix}$$

Step 4

Substitute π for x in the derivative function $f'(x) = \begin{pmatrix} (-\sin(x+\pi))\left(\frac{1}{4}e^{-2x^2+20}\right) \\ + \ (\cos(x+\pi))\left(-xe^{-2x^2+20}\right) \end{pmatrix}$, and solve for $f'(\pi)$.

$$f'(x) = \begin{pmatrix} (-\sin(x+\pi))\left(\frac{1}{4}e^{-2x^2+20}\right) \\ + \ (\cos(x+\pi))\left(-xe^{-2x^2+20}\right) \end{pmatrix}$$
$$f'(\pi) = \begin{pmatrix} (-\sin(\pi+\pi))\left(\frac{1}{4}e^{-2\pi^2+20}\right) \\ + \ (\cos(\pi+\pi))\left(-xe^{-2\pi^2+20}\right) \end{pmatrix}$$
$$f'(\pi) = \begin{pmatrix} (-\sin(2\pi))\left(\frac{1}{4}e^{-2\pi^2+20}\right) \\ + \ (\cos(2\pi))\left(-\pi e^{-2\pi^2+20}\right) \end{pmatrix}$$
$$f'(\pi) = (0)\left(\frac{1}{4}e^{0.260\,79\ldots}\right) + (1)\left(-\pi e^{0.260\,79\ldots}\right)$$
$$f'(\pi) = -\pi e^{0.260\,79\ldots}$$
$$f'(\pi) \approx -4.077\,65\ldots$$

Rounded to the nearest hundredth, $|f'(\pi)| = 4.08$.

34. WR

Step 1
Rearrange the equation $y - x - 1 = 0$ in the form $y = mx + b$.

$y - x - 1 = 0$
$y = x + 1$

Notice that the line has a slope of 1. For the tangent of the curve $y = 2xe^x$ to be parallel to the line, the derivative of $y = 2xe^x$ must be equal to 1.

Step 2
Apply the product rule to determine the derivative of $y = 2xe^x$.

$y = 2xe^x$
$y' = (2x)(e^x) + (2)(e^x)$
$y' = 2xe^x + 2e^x$
$y' = 2e^x(x + 1)$

Step 3
Substitute 1 for y' into the derivative $y' = 2e^x(x + 1)$, and bring all the terms to one side.

$y' = 2e^x(x + 1)$
$1 = 2e^x(x + 1)$
$0 = 2e^x(x + 1) - 1$

Step 4
Determine the value of x.
Using a graphing calculator, graph the equation $y = 2e^x(x + 1) - 1$ and determine the zero. On a TI-83 graphing calculator, the key strokes to find the the zeros of a function are as follows: press [2nd] [TRACE] and select 2:zero.
The graphing calculator will give the value of $-0.314\,9231$.
Therefore, $x = -0.314\,9231$ when the tangent line of the curve $y = 2xe^x$ is parallel to the line $y - x - 1 = 0$.

Step 5
Substitute $-0.314\,9231$ for x into the equation $y = 2xe^x$, and solve for y.

$y = 2xe^x$
$y = 2(-0.3149\ldots)e^{-0.3149\ldots}$
$y = -0.459\,66\ldots$

Therefore, the coordinates when the tangent line of the curve $y = 2xe^x$ is parallel to the line $y - x - 1 = 0$ is $(-0.31, -0.46)$, rounded to the nearest hundredth.

35. WR

Use the chain rule to find the derivative of $y = \sin(\sin x)$.

$$y = \sin(\sin x)$$
$$\frac{dy}{dx} = \cos(\sin x)\left(\frac{d}{dx}\sin x\right)$$
$$= \cos(\sin x)(\cos x)$$
$$= \cos^2 x(\sin x)$$

36. WR

Step 1
Determine $f'(x)$ and $g'(x)$.

$f(x) = \frac{1}{3}x^3$
$f'(x) = x^2$
$g(x) = -4x$
$g'(x) = -4$

Step 2
Determine $f'(x) + g'(x)$.

$f'(x) + g'(x) = x^2 - 4$

Step 3
Determine $(f + g)'(x)$.

$(f + g)(x) = f(x) + g(x)$
$= \frac{1}{3}x^3 - 4x$
$(f + g)'(x) = x^2 - 4$

Step 4
Sketch the graphs of $f'(x) + g'(x)$ and $(f + g)'(x)$.
The graphs of $f'(x) + g'(x)$ and $(f + g)'(x)$ are identical.

$f'(x) + g'(x) = x^2 - 4$
$(f + g)'(x) = x^2 - 4$

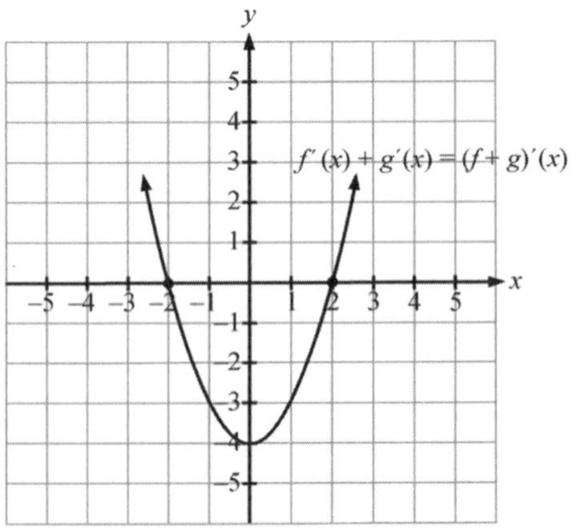

37. WR

Step 1

Rearrange the equation $2y - x + 1 = 0$ into the form $y = mx + b$.

$$\begin{aligned} 2y - x + 1 &= 0 \\ 2y &= x - 1 \\ y &= \frac{1}{2}x - \frac{1}{2} \end{aligned}$$

Step 2

Determine the slope of a line perpendicular to the line $y = \frac{1}{2}x - \frac{1}{2}$.

The slope of the line is $\frac{1}{2}$. To determine the slope of a perpendicular line, take the negative reciprocal of $\frac{1}{2}$. Therefore, the slope of a perpendicular line is as follows:

$$\begin{aligned} m_{\perp} &= \frac{1}{-\frac{1}{2}} \\ &= -2 \end{aligned}$$

Step 3

Determine the derivative of the function $f(x) = x^2 - 3$.

$$\begin{aligned} f(x) &= x^2 - 3 \\ f'(x) &= 2x \end{aligned}$$

The derivative of a function gives the slope of the tangent, so for the tangent line to be perpendicular to the line $2y - x + 1 = 0$, $f'(x) = -2$.

Step 4

Substitute -2 for $f'(x)$ into the equation $f'(x) = 2x$, and solve for x.

$$\begin{aligned} f'(x) &= 2x \\ -2 &= 2x \\ -1 &= x \end{aligned}$$

Step 5

Substitute -1 for x into the function $f(x) = x^2 - 3$, and solve for $f(-1)$.

$$\begin{aligned} f(x) &= x^2 - 3 \\ f(-1) &= (-1)^2 - 3 \\ f(-1) &= 1 - 3 \\ f(-1) &= -2 \end{aligned}$$

Therefore, the point on the graph of $f(x) = x^2 - 3$ where its tangent line is perpendicular to the line $2y - x + 1 = 0$ is $(-1, -2)$.

NOTES

Derivatives and their Applications

Derivatives and Their Applications

Table of Correlations

	Outcome	Practice Questions	Unit Test Questions	Practice Test 1	Practice Test 2
DER1.0	Connecting Graphs and Equations of Functions and Their Derivatives				
DER1.1	*sketch the graph of a derivative function, given the graph of a function that is continuous over an interval, and recognize points of inflection of the given function (i.e., points at which the concavity changes)*	1, 2, 3, 4	1, 2a, 2b		17
DER1.2	*recognize the second derivative as the rate of change of the rate of change (i.e., the rate of change of the slope of the tangent), and sketch the graphs of the first and second derivatives, given the graph of a smooth function*	5	3, 4, 5, 6	17	18
DER1.3	*determine algebraically the equation of the second derivative $f''(x)$ of a polynomial or simple rational function $f(x)$, and make connections, through investigation using technology, between the key features of the graph of the function (e.g., increasing/decreasing intervals, local maxima and minima, points of inflection, intervals of concavity) and corresponding features of the graphs of its first and second derivatives (e.g., for an increasing interval of the function, the first derivative is positive; for a point of inflection of the function, the slopes of tangents change their behaviour from increasing to decreasing or from decreasing to increasing, the first derivative has a maximum or minimum, and the second derivative is zero)*	6, 7, 8	7, 8, 9	18, 19, 20	19, 20, 21
DER1.4	*describe key features of a polynomial function, given information about its first and/or second derivatives (e.g., the graph of a derivative, the sign of a derivative over specific intervals, the x-intercepts of a derivative), sketch two or more possible graphs of the function that are consistent with the given information, and explain why an infinite number of graphs is possible*	9, 10, 11	10, 11	21, 22	22, 45
DER1.5	*sketch the graph of a polynomial function, given its equation, by using a variety of strategies (e.g., using the sign of the first derivative; using the sign of the second derivative; identifying even or odd functions) to determine its key features (e.g., increasing/ decreasing intervals, intercepts, local maxima and minima, points of inflection, intervals of concavity), and verify using technology*	12, 13, 14	12, 13, 14, 15	23, 24	23
DER2.0	Solving Problems Using Mathematical Models and Derivatives				
DER2.1	*make connections between the concept of motion (i.e., displacement, velocity, acceleration) and the concept of the derivative in a variety of ways (e.g., verbally, numerically, graphically, algebraically)*	15, 16, 17	16, 17, 18	25	24
DER2.2	*make connections between the graphical or algebraic representations of derivatives and real-world applications (e.g., population and rates of population change, prices and inflation rates, volume and rates of flow, height and growth rates)*	18, 19, 20	19, 20	26	25
DER2.3	*solve problems, using the derivative, that involve instantaneous rates of change, including problems arising from real-world applications (e.g., population growth, radioactive decay, temperature changes, hours of day-light, heights of tides), given the equation of a function**	21, 22, 23	21, 22a, 22b, 23, 24, 25	27	26

DER2.4	*solve optimization problems involving polynomial, simple rational, and exponential functions drawn from a variety of applications, including those arising from real-world situations*	24, 25, 26, 27	26, 27, 28	28, 29	27, 46
DER2.5	*solve problems arising from real-world applications by applying a mathematical model and the concepts and procedures associated with the derivative to determine mathematical results, and interpret and communicate the results*	28, 29, 30	29, 30, 31, 32	30	28

DER1.1 sketch the graph of a derivative function, given the graph of a function that is continuous over an interval, and recognize points of inflection of the given function (i.e., points at which the concavity changes)

DER1.2 recognize the second derivative as the rate of change of the rate of change (i.e., the rate of change of the slope of the tangent), and sketch the graphs of the first and second derivatives, given the graph of a smooth function

Graphing the First and Second Derivative Function

When the graph or type of a polynomial function is given, the first derivative function over a continuous interval can be sketched by approximating the slope of the graph, which is the slope of the tangent line, at various x-values.

A point on a graph of a function where the **concavity** of the graph changes from concave up to concave down, or vice versa, is called a **point of inflection**.

The points of inflection on the given graph are located at approximately $x = -2$ and $x = 0$.

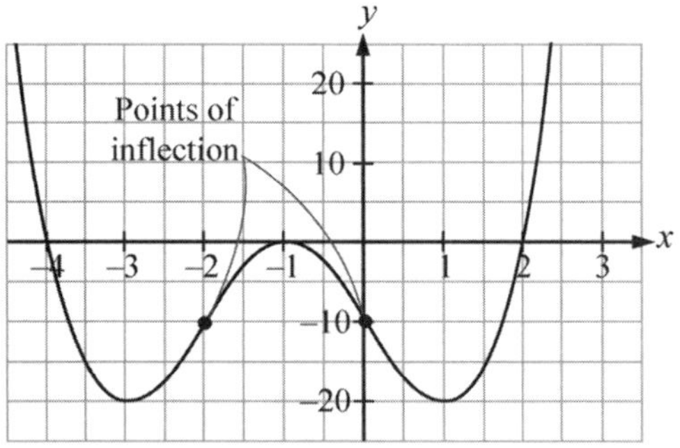

In the same way that the graph of the first derivative function of a given graph is sketched, the graph of the second derivative function can be drawn by approximating the slope of the graph of the first derivative function at various x-values.

Example

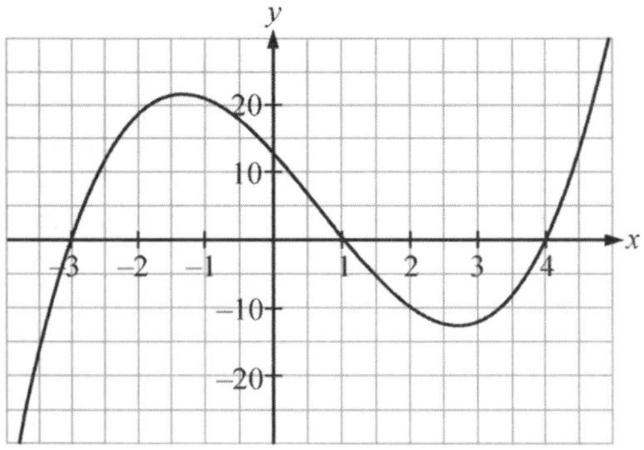

The graph of a cubic function is shown.

On the same set of axes, sketch the graphs of the first and second derivatives of the given cubic function.

Solution

Step 1

Analyze the slope of the graph from left to right using approximate x-values.

- When $x < -1.4$, the slope is positive and decreasing.
- When $x = -1.4$, the slope is 0.
- When $-1.4 < x < 0.7$, the slope is negative and decreasing.
- When $0.7 < x < 2.7$, the slope is negative and increasing.
- When $x = 2.7$, the slope is 0.
- When $x > 2.7$, the slope is positive and increasing.

Step 2

Graph the first derivative.

Graph the approximate slope values and the corresponding x-values on the same set of axes as the original function. Draw a smooth curve through these points to produce the curve shown here by the dotted line. Since the original graph is a cubic function, the first derivative is quadratic; thus, its graph is a parabola.

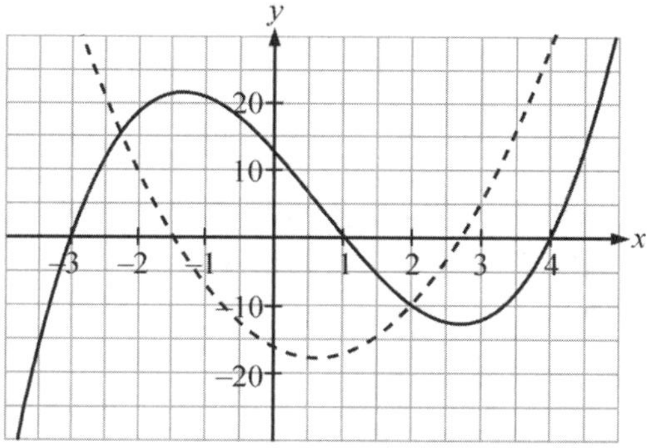

Step 3

Analyze the slope of the graph of the first derivative using approximate x-values.

- When $x = -3$, the slope is negative, such as -22.
- When $x < 0.7$ the slope is negative and increasing.
- When $x > 0.7$ the slope is positive and increasing.
- When $x = 4$, the slope is a positive number, such as $+20$.

Step 4

Graph the second derivative.

Notice that as the x-values of the graph increase, the slope of the graph increases. Therefore, because the graph of the first derivative is a parabola, the second derivative is a linear function.

Two points are required to graph a linear function. Notice that the slope of the first derivative is 0 when x is approximately 0.7, and the slope is approximately 20 when x is 4. Graph the points (0.7, 0) and (4, 20), and draw a straight line through these points to produce the graph shown here by the thick solid line. This graph is the second derivative of the original function.

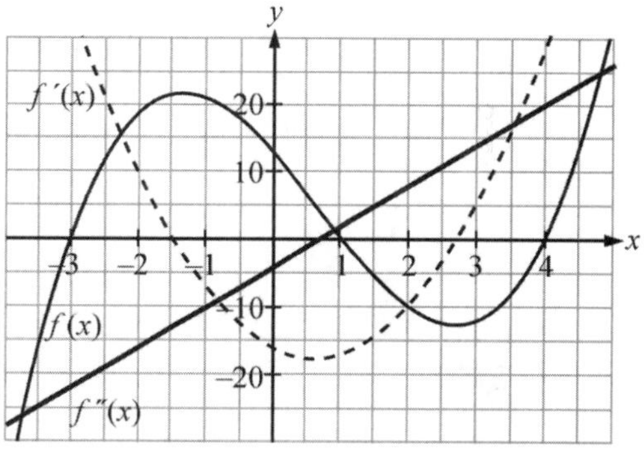

Use the following information to answer the next question.

The graph of $f(x)$ is shown.

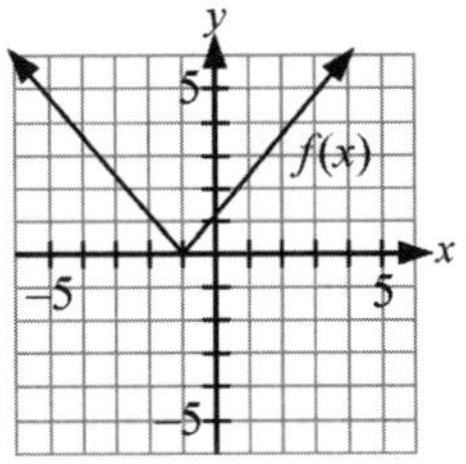

1. Which of the following graphs **best** represents the graph of $f'(x)$?

A.

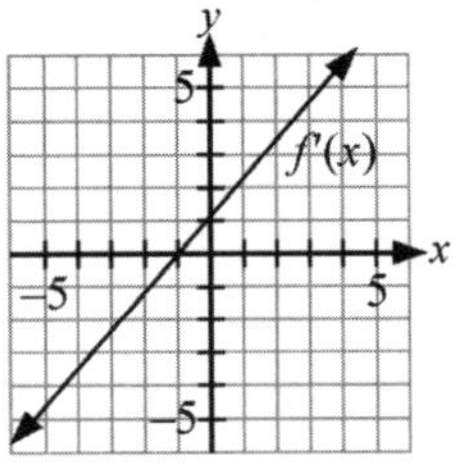

B.

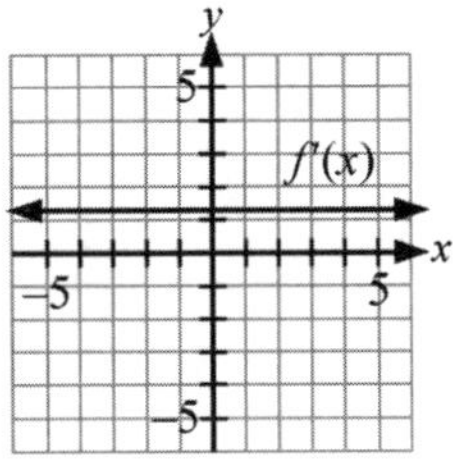

C.

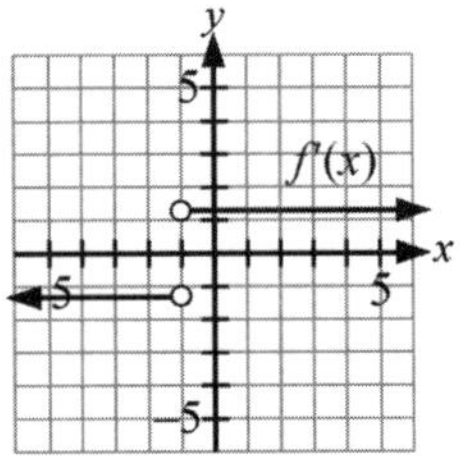

D.

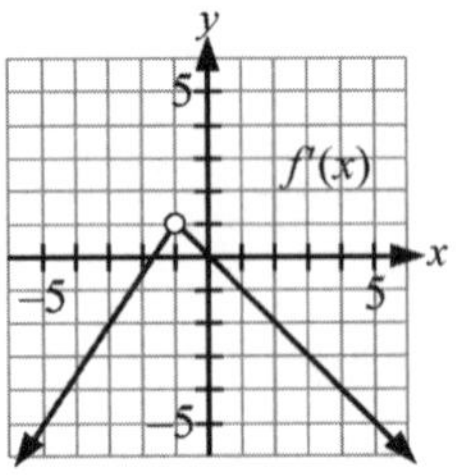

Use the following information to answer the next question.

The graph of the derivative of $f(x)$ is shown.

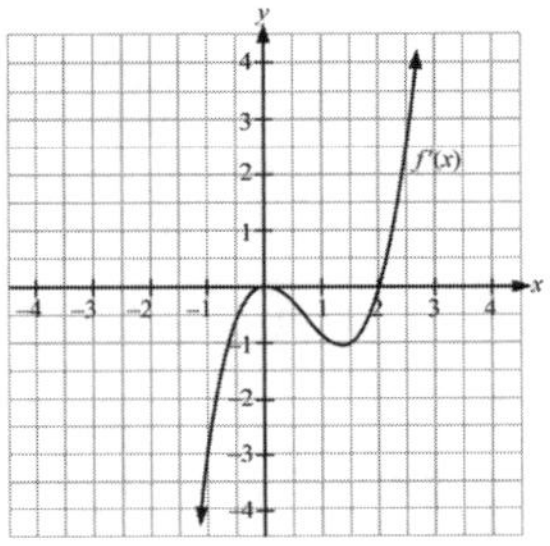

2. Which of the following graphs **best** approximates the graph of $f(x)$?

A.

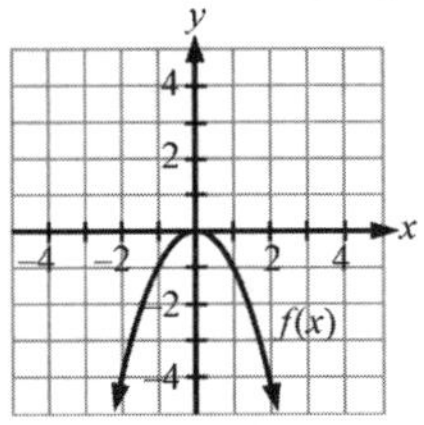

B.

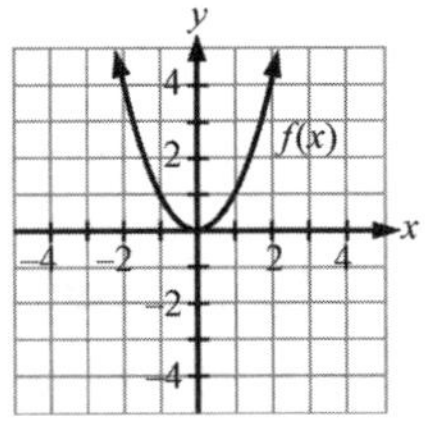

C.

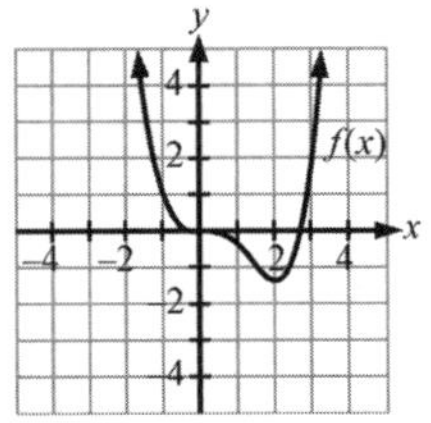

D.

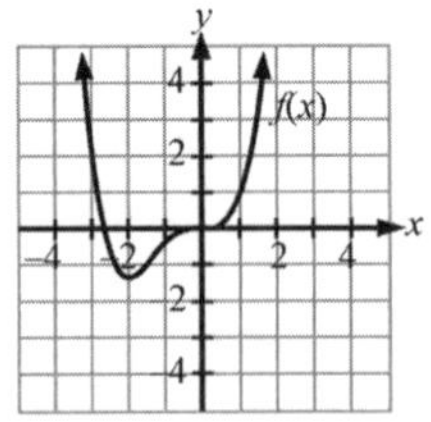

Use the following information to answer the next question.

The graph of $f(x)$ is shown.

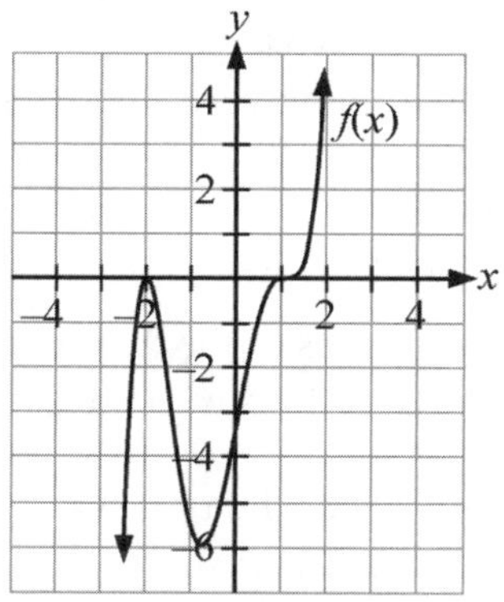

Written Response

3. Given the graph of $f(x)$, sketch the graph of $f'(x)$.

Written Response

4. A function $f(x)$ is not differentiable at $x = a$. If the graph of $f(x)$ were shown, what might be two of the reasons that are evident on the graph of $f(x)$ for this lack of differentiability at $x = a$?

Use the following information to answer the next question.

The graph of $y = f(x)$ is shown.

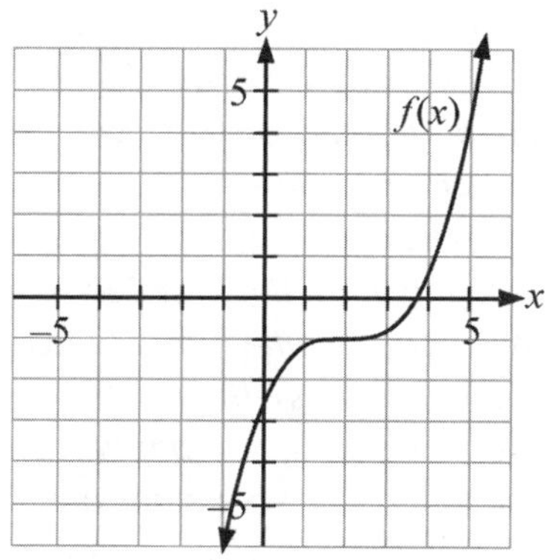

5. For what approximate value of x is the instantaneous rate of change of $f(x)$ equal to 0?

   A. 0 **B.** 0.7

   C. 2.0 **D.** 3.3

DER1.3 determine algebraically the equation of the second derivative f''(x) of a polynomial or simple rational function f(x), and make connections, through investigation using technology, between the key features of the graph of the function (e.g., increasing/decreasing intervals, local maxima and minima, points of inflection, intervals of concavity) and corresponding features of the graphs of its first and second derivatives (e.g., for an increasing interval of the function, the first derivative is positive; for a point of inflection of the function, the slopes of tangents change their behaviour from increasing to decreasing or from decreasing to increasing, the first derivative has a maximum or minimum, and the second derivative is zero)

DER1.4 describe key features of a polynomial function, given information about its first and/or second derivatives (e.g., the graph of a derivative, the sign of a derivative over specific intervals, the x-intercepts of a derivative), sketch two or more possible graphs of the function that are consistent with the given information, and explain why an infinite number of graphs is possible

DER1.5 sketch the graph of a polynomial function, given its equation, by using a variety of strategies (e.g., using the sign of the first derivative; using the sign of the second derivative; identifying even or odd functions) to determine its key features (e.g., increasing/ decreasing intervals, intercepts, local maxima and minima, points of inflection, intervals of concavity), and verify using technology

Sketching a Polynomial Function Given its First and Second Derivative

The first and second derivative of a polynomial function can be used to determine key features of the graph of the function. The second derivative is the derivative of the first derivative. Once the key features of the polynomial function are found, the graph of the function can be sketched.

The graph of a polynomial function can be sketched given the equations or graphs of its first and second derivative.

When sketching the graph of a polynomial function from the graphs of its first and second derivative, translating the graph of a function vertically does not change the graph of the derivative. Conversely, if the graph of the derivative is given, the graph of the original function may be any one of an infinite family of functions that are vertical translations of each other. Knowing one point on the graph of the function will specify which function is required.

The following features of the function, $f(x)$, can be determined and used to sketch the graph:

- The function is odd when $f(-x) = -f(x)$ or even when $f(-x) = f(x)$.
- The function approaches positive or negative infinity for extreme positive or negative x-values.
- For the x-intercepts, set $f(x) = 0$ and solve for x.
- For the y-intercept, set $x = 0$ and solve for $f(x)$.
- Intervals of increase and decrease occur when $f'(x) > 0$ and $f'(x) < 0$, respectively.
- Flattening of the slope, usually local maximums and minimums, occurs when $f'(x) = 0$.
- The points of inflection occur when $f''(x) = 0$.
- The function is concave up when $f''(x) > 0$ and concave down when $f''(x) < 0$.

6. The first derivative of a rational expression is defined by $f'(x) = -\frac{4}{x^2}$.

Which of the following statements about the graph of $f(x)$ is **true**?

A. The function $f(x)$ is concave up for all real values of x.

B. The function $f(x)$ is concave up on the interval $-\infty < x < 0$.

C. The function $f(x)$ is concave down on the interval $0 < x < \infty$.

D. The function $f(x)$ is concave down on the interval $-\infty < x < 0$.

Written Response

7. Using the first and second derivative of the function $f(x) = x^4 - 2x^3$, determine the maximum or minimum point or points and the intervals of concavity.

Written Response

8. Determine the first and second derivatives of the function
$f(x) = x^{10} - 2x^7 + 3x^4 - 6x - 9.$

Use the following information to answer the next question.

Information about a particular polynomial function, $f(x)$, where $x \in \mathbb{R}$, is provided in the given table.

x	$f(x)$	$f'(x)$	$f''(x)$
-1	$-\frac{5}{3}$	$+$	$-$
1	$\frac{5}{3}$	0	$-$
3	1	0	$+$
4	$\frac{5}{3}$	$\frac{3}{2}$	$+$

9. Which of the following conclusions can be made about the graph of $f(x)$ at $x = 4$?
   A. The graph is increasing and concave up.
   B. The graph is decreasing and concave up.
   C. The graph is increasing, and there is a point of inflection.
   D. The graph is decreasing, and there is a point of inflection.

Use the following information to answer the next question.

The graph of $f'(x)$ the derivative of a function $f(x)$, is shown.

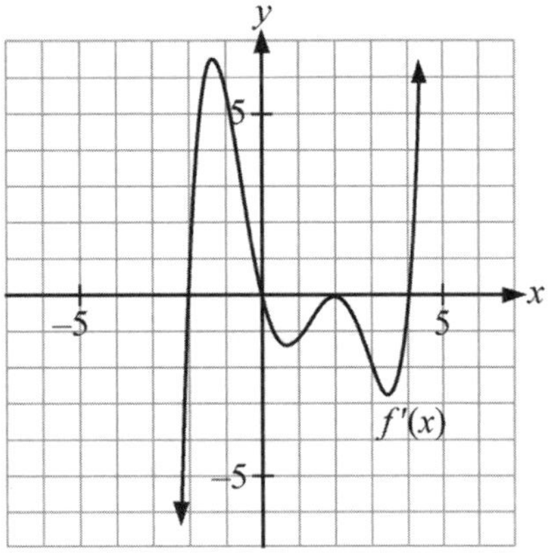

10. On approximately which of the following intervals is the graph of $f(x)$ increasing?

A. $-2 < x < 0$ and $4 < x < \infty$

B. $0 < x < 2$ and $5 < x < \infty$

C. $-\infty < x < -1$ and $1 < x < 2$

D. $2.5 < x < 4$ and $5.5 < x < \infty$

Written Response

11. How does knowing the x-intercepts of the graph of the derivative of a polynomial function help to sketch the graph of the function itself?

12. One conclusion that can be reached when the second derivative of a polynomial function is equal to zero at $x = a$ is that the function

A. is concave down at $x = a$

B. has an x-intercept at $x = a$

C. has a local maximum at $x = a$

D. may have a point of inflection at $x = a$

Numerical Response

13. Calculated to the nearest hundredth, the y-coordinate of the local maximum of the function $f(x) = 2x^3 + \frac{1}{2}x^2 - 2x + 9$ is ________.

Use the following information to answer the next question.

A curve can be defined by the following characteristics:

- Odd or even
- y-intercepts and x-intercepts
- Intervals of increase or decrease
- Local extrema
- Points of inflection
- Intervals of concavity

Written Response

14. Explain the curve defined by $f(x) = -\frac{4}{3}x^3 + 4x^2 - 3x$ according to the given characteristics, and use this information to sketch a graph of $f(x)$.

DER2.1 make connections between the concept of motion (i.e., displacement, velocity, acceleration) and the concept of the derivative in a variety of ways (e.g., verbally, numerically, graphically, algebraically)

Making Connections between the Concepts of Motion and Derivatives

If a car is travelling due north on a straight road, the car's speedometer gives its instantaneous velocity in a northward direction at any particular time.

Instantaneous velocity is the instantaneous rate of change of displacement with respect to time. If the driver of the car accelerates, then the instantaneous acceleration is the instantaneous rate of change of velocity with respect to time.

Displacement is defined as the net change in position of an object from start to finish. In other words, displacement refers to how far away an object is when it finishes moving relative to where it started. If displacement from a starting point, s, is defined by a function of time, t so that $s = f(t)$, then the instantaneous velocity, v, at any time is the derivative of the displacement with respect to time. This can be expressed in the formula

$$v = \frac{ds}{dt} = f'(t).$$

The instantaneous acceleration at any time, a, is the instantaneous rate of change of the velocity, which is the derivative of the velocity with respect to time. This is also the second derivative of the displacement function. This can be expressed in the formula $a = \frac{dv}{dt} = \frac{d^2s}{dt^2} = f''(t)$.

15. Which of the following position functions has a constant acceleration?

A. $s(t) = 2t^2 - 9t + 7$

B. $s(t) = 7t^3 - 4t^2 - 3t$

C. $s(t) = 3t^3 - 5t^2 + 4t - 1$

D. $s(t) = 5t^4 - 4t^3 + 4t - 3$

Use the following information to answer the next question.

The displacement-time graph of an object is shown and is divided into six stages.

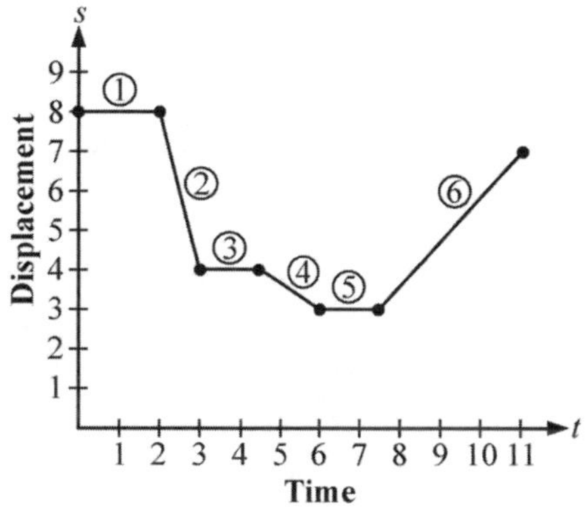

16. On which stage is the magnitude of the velocity the greatest?

A. 1 **B.** 2

C. 4 **D.** 6

Use the following information to answer the next question.

A rock is thrown vertically upward from ground level with an initial velocity of 30 m/s. At some point, the rock stops travelling upward and falls back toward the ground. The height, h, in metres, of the rock is a function of the time, t, in seconds, defined as $h(t) = -5t^2 + 30t$, where $t \geq 0$.

Numerical Response

17. To the nearest metre, the maximum height reached by the rock is __________ m.

DER2.2 make connections between the graphical or algebraic representations of derivatives and real-world applications (e.g., population and rates of population change, prices and inflation rates, volume and rates of flow, height and growth rates)

CONNECTING REPRESENTATIONS OF DERIVATIVES IN REAL-WORLD SITUATIONS

There are numerous real-world situations where it is important to know and understand historical, current, and predicted rates of change.
Since derivatives are measurements of instantaneous rates of change, working with rates of change often involves analyzing, calculating, estimating, and graphing derivatives.

Example

A particular species of fish grows in length for the first two weeks after birth at a rate measured in millimetres per day given by $L\ (d) = 0.06\pi d^2$, in which d is the number of days after birth.

Explain why $L\ (d)$ is a formula for a derivative and how it is a derivative of a quantity with respect to another quantity.

Solution

The formula is a derivative because it is a rate of change formula.

Because the formula involves a change in length given in millimetres, over a period of time in days, the formula is a derivative of length with respect to time.

What is the degree of the function that has the derivative $L\ (d) = 0.06\pi d^2$?

Solution

The power rule of derivatives states that if $f(x) = x^n$, in which n is a natural number, then the derivative is $f'(x) = nx^{n-1}$. From the power rule of derivatives, the original function has a degree of n, and the derivative function has a degree of $n - 1$, in which n is a natural number.
Since the derivative function, $L\ (d) = 0.06\pi d^2$, has a degree of 2, then the degree of the original function is found as follows:
$2 = n - 1$
$n = 3$

Therefore, the degree of the function that has the derivative $L\ (d) = 0.06\pi d^2$ is 3.

Rounded to the nearest day, what number of days results in a growth rate that is 10 mm/day?

Solution

If the growth rate is 10 mm/day, solve for d when $L\ (d) = 10$.

$$\begin{aligned} L\ (d) &= 0.06\pi d^2 \\ 10 &= 0.06\pi d^2 \\ \frac{10}{0.06\pi} &= d^2 \\ \sqrt{\frac{10}{0.06\pi}} &= d \\ 7 &\approx d \end{aligned}$$

Therefore, the growth rate is 10 mm/day by the seventh day.

How would doubling the number of days after birth affect the growth rate?

Solution

Determine the growth rate if the number of days were doubled from d to $2d$.

$$\begin{aligned} L\ (d) &= 0.06\pi d^2 \\ L_2(d) &= 0.06\pi(2d)^2 \\ &= 4(0.06\pi d^2) \\ &= 4L\ (d) \end{aligned}$$

Doubling the number of days would quadruple the growth rate.

Use the following information to answer the next question.

Gasoline is leaking from a fuel truck at a rate of $R(t) = 2\ 000e^{-0.2t}$ gal/h, where t represents the time in hours.

18. The rate of leakage first drops below 225 gal/h after approximately

A. 1.2 h **B.** 2.9 h

C. 5.7 h **D.** 10.9 h

Use the following information to answer the next question.

A tank with a capacity of 5 000 L drains completely in 40 min. The graph provided shows the volume of water remaining in the tank after draining for t min.

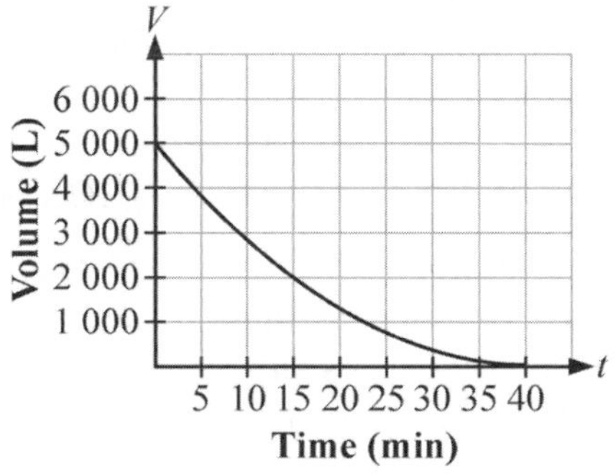

19. At which of the following times is the rate of drainage the greatest?

A. 5 min **B.** 15 min

C. 25 min **D.** 35 min

Use the following information to answer the next question.

A bacteria culture grows at a rate proportional to its population. The growth rate, in bacteria/h, of the culture of bacteria is given by the function $g(t) = 1\ 000(2.5)^{\frac{t}{2}}$, in which t is the time measured in hours.

Numerical Response

20. To the nearest whole number, what is the rate of growth of the bacteria culture after 5 h? __________ bacteria/h

*DER2.3 solve problems, using the derivative, that involve instantaneous rates of change, including problems arising from real-world applications (e.g., population growth, radioactive decay, temperature changes, hours of day-light, heights of tides), given the equation of a function**

Solving Instantaneous Rate of Change Problems

If a known function describes a real-world quantity in terms of an independent variable, such as time, the derivative will give the rate of change of that quantity with respect to the independent variable. The derivative can be used to determine the instantaneous rate of change of the quantity for any particular value of the independent variable.

Example

The future size of the population of a particular species of birds in northern Ontario can be estimated by the formula $P = \dfrac{8\ 000}{1 + 53(0.3)^t}$, in which t is the time in years.

Rounded to the nearest whole number, determine the rate of growth of the population after 7 yr using the derivative.

Solution

Find the derivative to determine the rate of growth of the population after t years.

Step 1

In order to find the derivative, write the quotient, $\dfrac{8\ 000}{1 + 53(0.3)^t}$, as a product.

$P = 8\ 000\left(1 + 53(0.3)^t\right)^{-1}$

Step 2

Find the derivative of $P = 8\ 000\left(1 + 53(0.3)^t\right)^{-1}$ using the derivative rules.

The derivative of $(0.3)^t$ is $(0.3)^t \ln 0.3$.

$P = 8\ 000\left(1 + 53(0.3)^t\right)^{-1}$

$\dfrac{dP}{dt} = 8\ 000(-1)\left(1 + 53(0.3)^t\right)^{-2}$

$\left(0 + 53(0.3)^t \ln 0.3\right)$

$= -8\ 000\left(1 + 53(0.3)^t\right)^{-2}\left(53(0.3)^t \ln 0.3\right)$

Step 3

Calculate $\frac{dP}{dt}$ when $t = 7$.

$\frac{dP}{dt} = -8\,000\left(1+53(0.3)^7\right)^{-2}\left(53(0.3)^7 \ln 0.3\right)$

Using a calculator, the result is approximately 109.1.

After 7 yr, the population is growing at a rate of approximately 109 birds/yr.

---

21. The electric potential (voltage) of a battery that is dying is given by the equation $P = 10 - (0.04)t^2$, where t is the time elapsed in hours. What is the rate of change of the electric potential of the battery after 3 h?

A. –37.5 V/h

B. –0.24 V/h

C. 9.64 V/h

D. 13.23 V/h

Use the following information to answer the next question.

The volume of water in a certain cylindrical tank is increasing at a rate of 80 cm^3/min, and the radius of the tank is 12 cm.

22. The rate of change of the height with respect to time of the given cylindrical tank, to the nearest hundredth, is

A. 0.18 cm/min **B.** 1.06 cm/min

C. 1.75 cm/min **D.** 2.12 cm/min

Use the following information to answer the next question.

Wind chill is the temperature determined from a combination of the actual air temperature and wind speed. For an air temperature of 32, the wind chill, W, in degrees Fahrenheit, is given by the function $W(s) = 55.6 - 22.1s^{0.16}$, where s is the wind speed in mi/h.

Numerical Response

23. To the nearest hundredth, at what rate is the wind chill decreasing when the wind speed is 20 mi/h? __________°F/h

DER2.4 solve optimization problems involving polynomial, simple rational, and exponential functions drawn from a variety of applications, including those arising from real-world situations

Solving Optimization Problems

An optimization problem involves finding the preferred or optimum amount of a specific quantity. If a function represents an application involving optimization, the optimum quantity or amount occurs at either the relative maximum or minimum or at the end values of the function.

The following steps can be taken to solve optimization problems:

1. Find the derivative of the function, $f(x)$.
2. Determine the potential local maximum or minimum by setting $f'(x) = 0$.
3. If necessary, such as for maximum revenue questions, substitute the local maximum value into $f(x)$ to determine the maximum value desired.

Use the following information to answer the next question.

A wire with a length of 30 cm is cut into two pieces. One piece is bent into the shape of a square. The other piece is bent into the shape of a rectangle whose length is twice its width. The relationship between the lengths of wire for the two shapes is given by $30 = 4x + 6y$, in which x is the width of the square and y is the width of the rectangle, both in metres. The sum of the areas of the square and the rectangle is given by $A = x^2 + 2y^2$. The sum is also a minimum.

24. What is the length of the longer piece of wire, to the nearest tenth of a metre?

A. 2.6 m **B.** 3.5 m

C. 14.1 m **D.** 15.9 m

Use the following information to answer the next question.

The cost of producing x amount of dolls is defined by the function $C(x) = 4x^2 - 64x + 381$.

Numerical Response

25. How many dolls are produced when the cost is at a minimum? __________

Use the following information to answer the next question.

The equation $P = xy^3$ represents the product of one positive number, x, and the cube of another positive number, y.

Written Response

26. If the sum of the two numbers is 12, find the numbers that would yield a maximum product, P.

Use the following information to answer the next question.

A certain courier company will only accept cylindrical packages whose height and circumference combined do not exceed 10 ft.

Written Response

27. What must the height of the cylindrical package be to maximize its volume if the volume of a cylinder is given by $V = \pi r^2 h$, in which V represents the volume in cubic feet, r represents the radius in feet, and h represents the height in feet?

DER2.5 solve problems arising from real-world applications by applying a mathematical model and the concepts and procedures associated with the derivative to determine mathematical results, and interpret and communicate the results

Solving Problems Using Mathematical Models

It is a common practice in many fields of study to attempt to describe changing situations with mathematical models. Because rates of change or maximums and minimums are often of interest in these situations, the mathematics usually involve finding the derivative. The models are seldom one hundred percent accurate, but they are usually good estimates for particular values of the independent variable.

Example

Factories A and B are 10 km apart. Factory B emits four times the pollutants into the air as factory A. The number, N, of particles of pollutants in the air from a given factory is inversely proportional to the square of the distance from that factory $\left(y = \dfrac{k}{f(x)}\right)$.

John and Irene want to build a house adjacent to a straight road that connects the two factories. They want the house to be located at the point at which the pollution from the factories is the least.

How far from factory A, to the nearest tenth of a kilometre, should John and Irene build their house in order to experience the minimum amount of pollution from the two factories? Explain your answer.

Solution

Step 1

Determine a function that represents the total number of particles emitted by both factories.

- Let x be the distance from the house to factory A.
- Let $(10 - x)$ be the distance from the house to factory B.

The number of particles from factory A is $\dfrac{k}{x^2}$, and the number of particles from factory B is $\dfrac{4k}{(10-x)^2}$.

The total number of particles of pollution at the house would be $N = \dfrac{k}{x^2} + \dfrac{4k}{(10-x)^2}$.

Step 2

Determine the derivative of N with respect to x.

$$N = \frac{k}{x^2} + \frac{4k}{(10-x)^2}$$

$$N = kx^{-2} + 4k(10-x)^{-2}$$

$$\frac{dN}{dx} = -2kx^{-3} + \left(-8k(10-x)^{-3}\right)(-1)$$

$$\frac{dN}{dx} = -2kx^{-3} + 8k(10-x)^{-3}$$

The derivative of N with respect to x is $-2kx^{-3} + 8k(10-x)^{-3}$.

Step 3

Determine the minimum amount of pollution particles using the derivative.

The minimum amount of pollution will occur when $\frac{dN}{dx} = 0$.

$$-2kx^{-3} + 8k(10-x)^{-3} = 0$$
$$8k(10-x)^{-3} = 2kx^{-3}$$
$$\frac{4}{(10-x)^3} = \frac{1}{x^3}$$
$$4x^3 = (10-x)^3$$
$$\sqrt[3]{4}x = 10 - x$$
$$\sqrt[3]{4}x + x = 10$$
$$x(\sqrt[3]{4} + 1) = 10$$
$$x = \frac{10}{(\sqrt[3]{4} + 1)}$$
$$x \approx 3.9$$

Therefore, John and Irene should build their house approximately 3.9 km from factory A. The answer is a minimum because the pollution would increase as you get closer to either of the factories.

You can see this from the form of the function $N = \frac{k}{x^2} + \frac{4k}{(10-x)^2}$ because as the denominators of the rational expressions approach 0, their values approach infinity.

Use the following information to answer the next question.

> A bacterial culture begins with 1 000 bacteria, and after 4 h, the count is 5 000. The bacterial culture grows according to the equation $C(t) = Ae^{kt}$, where A is the initial number of bacteria in the culture, k is a constant, and t is the time in hours.

28. Rounded to the nearest whole number, what is the rate of growth of the bacterial culture after 5 h?

A. 3 008 bacteria/h

B. 3 009 bacteria/h

C. 7 476 bacteria/h

D. 7 477 bacteria/h

Use the following information to answer the next question.

> The velocity of a flowing river at a popular picnic area is modelled by the function $v(t) = 32 + 5\sin(\sqrt{t} + 5)$, $0 \le t \le 68$, where $v(t)$ is the velocity measured in m/min and t is the time in minutes.

29. If a swimmer jumps into the water and begins swimming against the current at a constant rate of 85 m/min, his rate of acceleration in the water after 10 min will be approximately

A. -28.66 m/min^2

B. -0.48 m/min^2

C. 0.48 m/min^2

D. 56.34 m/min^2

Use the following information to answer the next question.

After having been shaped by using heat, a piece of metal with a temperature of 1 500°C must be dropped into a tank of water to cool. The tank of water is kept at a temperature of 35°C. After 10 min in the cooling tank, the metal's temperature drops to 750°C. The rate of decrease in the metal's temperature is said to be negligible when the metal reaches 75°C, so the metal is removed from the tank when it reaches this temperature.
The change in temperature of the piece of metal follows Newton's law of cooling, which states that the difference in temperature between an object and its surroundings decreases exponentially according to the relationship $T - T_s = (T_0 - T_s)e^{kt}$, where T is the object's temperature at time t, T_s is the the temperature of the surroundings, T_0 is the initial temperature of the object, and k is a constant representing the relative rate of cooling of the given object.

Numerical Response

30. To the nearest hundredth, what is the negligible rate of temperature decrease for this particular metal? __________°C/min

Answers and Solutions
Derivatives and their Applications

1. C	**7. WR**	**13. 9.96**	**19. A**	**25. 8**
2. C	**8. WR**	**14. WR**	**20. 9882**	**26. WR**
3. WR	**9. A**	**15. A**	**21. B**	**27. WR**
4. WR	**10. A**	**16. B**	**22. A**	**28. A**
5. C	**11. WR**	**17. 45**	**23. 0.29**	**29. C**
6. D	**12. D**	**18. D**	**24. D**	**30. 2.87**

1. C

On the graph of $f(x)$, there is an abrupt change in slope at $x = -1$. Therefore, the derivative graph will be undefined at $x = -1$.

To the left of $x = -1$, the slope is constant at $\frac{4-0}{-4.3-(-1)} \approx -1.2$. Therefore, on the derivative graph $f'(x)$, there is a horizontal line at $y = -1.2$ defined on the interval $-\infty < x < -1$.

To the right of $x = -1$, the slope is constant at $\frac{4-0}{2.3-(-1)} \approx 1.2$. Therefore, on the derivative graph $f'(x)$, there is a horizontal line at $y = 1.2$ defined on the interval $-1 < x < \infty$.

Graph C best represents the graph of $f'(x)$.

2. C

Analyze the y-values from left to right of the graph of the derivative.

- $-\infty < x < 0$, y-values are negative and increasing
- $x = 0$, y-value is zero
- $0 < x < 1.4$, y-values are negative and decreasing
- $1.4 < x < 2$, y-values are negative and increasing
- $x = 2$, y-value is zero
- $2 < x < \infty$, y-values are positive and increasing

Since the y-values of the graph of the derivative are equal to the slopes of $f(x)$, the following slope values should occur in the graph of $f(x)$:

- $-\infty < x < 0$, slope is negative and increasing
- $x = 0$, slope is zero
- $0 < x < 1.4$, slope is negative and decreasing
- $1.4 < x < 2$, slope is negative and increasing
- $x = 2$, slope is zero
- $2 < x < \infty$, slope is positive and increasing

The graph in alternative C is the only graph that shows these slope values.

3. WR

Step 1
Analyze the slope of the graph, when it is viewed from left to right, using approximate x-values.

- $x < -2$, the slope is positive and decreasing
- $x = -2$, the slope is 0
- $-2 < x < -1.4$, the slope is negative and decreasing
- $x = -1.4$ is a point of inflection
- $-1.4 < x < -0.9$, the slope is negative and increasing
- $x = -0.9$, the slope is 0
- $-0.9 < x < 0$, the slope is positive and increasing
- $x = 0$ is a point of inflection
- $0 < x < 1$, the slope is positive and decreasing
- $x = 1$, the slope is 0
- $x > 1$, the slope is positive and increasing

Step 2
Graph the approximate slope values. Connect the points using a thick line. The resulting graph is the derivative of the function.

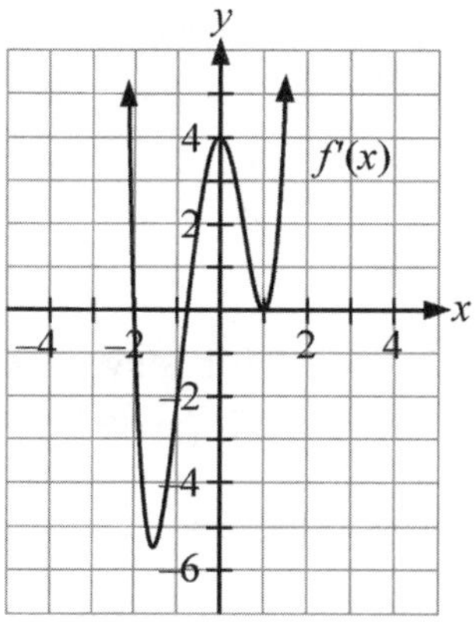

4. WR

The function $f(x)$ may be undefined at $x = a$. The graph would have a vertical asymptote or a hole at $x = a$.

The derivative of the function may be undefined at $x = a$. The graph might have a cusp or an endpoint at $x = a$.

The function may be a piecewise function. The graph of $f(x)$ would show a break and not be continuous at $x = a$.

5. C

The instantaneous rate of change is equal to 0 when the slope of the tangent is equal to 0 on the graph of $f(x)$. At approximately $x = 2.0$, the slope of the tangent is equal to 0.

Therefore, the instantaneous rate of change of $f(x)$ is equal to 0 at approximately $x = 2.0$.

6. D

Step 1
Determine the second derivative of the function $f(x)$.

$$f'(x) = -\frac{4}{x^2}$$
$$f'(x) = -4x^{-2}$$
$$f''(x) = 8x^{-3}$$

Step 2
Determine the x-coordinate of the inflection point.

Solve for x when $f''(x) = 0$.

$$f''(x) = 8x^{-3}$$
$$0 = 8x^{-3}$$
$$0 = x^{-3}$$
$$x = 0$$

Step 3
Determine the intervals of concavity.

Substitute any value greater than 0 into $f''(x)$, and solve.

Let $x = 1$.

$$f''(x) = 8x^{-3}$$
$$f''(1) = 8(1)^{-3}$$
$$= 8$$

The function $f''(x)$ is positive on the interval $x > 0$. Therefore, $f(x)$ is concave up on the interval $0 < x < \infty$.

Substitute any value less than 0 into $f''(x)$, and solve.

Let $x = -1$.

$$f''(x) = 8x^{-3}$$
$$f''(-1) = 8(-1)^{-3}$$
$$= -8$$

The function $f''(x)$ is negative on the interval $x < 0$. Therefore, $f(x)$ is concave down on the interval $-\infty < x < 0$.

7. WR

Determine the values of x when $f'(0) = 0$.

$$f(x) = x^4 - 2x^3$$
$$f'(x) = 4x^3 - 6x^2$$
$$0 = 2x^2(2x - 3)$$
$$x = 0, \frac{3}{2}$$

Using test points on either side of $x = 0$ and $x = \frac{3}{2}$ reveals that the first derivative is negative on the interval $-\infty < x < \frac{3}{2}$ and positive on the interval $\frac{3}{2} < x < \infty$. A negative first derivative on a given interval corresponds to a decreasing function on that interval. Similarly, a positive first derivative on a given interval corresponds to an increasing function on that interval. Therefore, the graph of $f(x)$ is decreasing on the interval $-\infty < x < \frac{3}{2}$ and increasing on the interval $\frac{3}{2} < x < \infty$.

In addition, at the point where the first derivative of a function is equal to zero and changes sign from negative to positive, the function has a local minimum. For the function $f(x)$, a local minimum occurs at $x = \frac{3}{2}$ of $f\left(\frac{3}{2}\right) = -\frac{27}{16}$.

Determine the values of x when $f''(x) = 0$.

$$f'(x) = 4x^3 - 6x^2$$
$$f''(x) = 12x^2 - 12x$$
$$0 = 12x(x - 1)$$
$$x = 0, 1$$

Using test points on either side of $x = 0$ and $x = 1$ reveals that the second derivative is negative on the interval $0 < x < 1$ and positive on the intervals $-\infty < x < 0$ and $1 < x < \infty$. A negative second derivative on a given interval corresponds to a function that is concave down on that interval. Similarly, a positive second derivative on a given interval corresponds to function that is concave up on that interval. Therefore, the graph of $f(x)$ is concave down on $0 < x < 1$ and concave up on $-\infty < x < 0$ and $1 < x < \infty$.

In addition, at the point where the second derivative of a function is equal to zero and changes sign from negative to positive or positive to negative, the graph of the function moves from concave down to concave up or concave up to concave down, resulting in points of inflection where $f''(x) = 0$. On the graph of $f(x)$, points of inflection occur at $x = 0$ and $x = 1$ of $(0, f(0)) = (0, 1)$ and $(1, f(1)) = (1, -1)$.

8. WR

Step 1
Determine the first derivative of the function.

$f(x) = x^{10} - 2x^7 + 3x^4 - 6x - 9$
$f'(x) = 10x^9 - 14x^6 + 12x^3 - 6$

Step 2
Determine the second derivative of the function.

$f'(x) = 10x^9 - 14x^6 + 12x^3 - 6$
$f''(x) = 90x^8 - 84x^5 + 36x^2$

9. A

At $x = 4$, $f'(x)$ is positive; therefore, the function $f(x)$ is increasing.

At $x = 4$, $f''(x)$ is also positive; therefore, the function $f(x)$ is concave up at $x = 4$.

10. A

The graph of $f(x)$ is increasing on intervals where the graph of $f'(x)$ is positive.

Observing the given graph, $f'(x)$ is positive on the intervals $-2 < x < 0$ and $4 < x < \infty$.

Therefore, the graph of $f(x)$ is increasing on the intervals $-2 < x < 0$ and $4 < x < \infty$.

11. WR

The coordinates of the x-intercepts of the derivative function correspond to the x-coordinates of local extrema on the graph of the function itself.
More information is required about the first derivative in order to conclude whether the extrema are local maxima or local minima.

12. D

When the second derivative function is equal to zero at a particular point, then there is a point of inflection on the original function at that point. Thus, when the second derivative graph of a polynomial function is equal to zero at $x = a$, there is a point of inflection on the function graph at $x = a$.

13. 9.96

Step 1
Find the first derivative of the function $f(x)$.

$f(x) = 2x^3 + \frac{1}{2}x^2 - 2x + 9$
$f'(x) = 6x^2 + x - 2$

Step 2
Determine the intervals where the function is increasing and decreasing.
Solve for x when $f(x) = 0$.

$$\begin{aligned} f'(x) &= 6x^2 + x - 2 \\ 0 &= 6x^2 + x - 2 \\ 0 &= 6x^2 + 4x - 3x - 2 \\ 0 &= 2x(3x+2) - 1(3x+2) \\ 0 &= (2x-1)(3x+2) \end{aligned}$$

$2x - 1 = 0$
$x = \frac{1}{2}$

$3x + 2 = 0$
$x = \frac{-2}{3}$

Test interval $-\infty < x < \frac{-2}{3}$.

$$\begin{aligned} f'(x) &= 6x^2 + x - 2 \\ f'(-1) &= 6(-1)^2 + (-1) - 2 \\ &= 3 \end{aligned}$$

Test interval $\frac{-2}{3} < x < \frac{1}{2}$.

$$\begin{aligned} f'(x) &= 6x^2 + x - 2 \\ f'(0) &= 6(0)^2 + (0) - 2 \\ &= -2 \end{aligned}$$

Test interval $\frac{1}{2} < x < \infty$.

$$\begin{aligned} f'(x) &= 6x^2 + x - 2 \\ f'(1) &= 6(1)^2 + (1) - 2 \\ &= 5 \end{aligned}$$

The given table summarizes the behaviour of the function.

Interval	$f'(x)$	Increasing / Decreasing
$-\infty < x < \frac{-2}{3}$	+	Increasing
$\frac{-2}{3} < x < \frac{1}{2}$	–	Decreasing
$\frac{1}{2} < x < \infty$	+	Increasing

Step 3
Determine the local maximum point.

The derivative is positive to the left of $x = -\frac{2}{3}$ and negative to the right of $x = -\frac{2}{3}$. Therefore, there is a local maximum at $x = -\frac{2}{3}$.

Solve $f(x)$ when $x = -\frac{2}{3}$.

$$f(x) = 2x^3 + \frac{1}{2}x^2 - 2x + 9$$
$$f\left(-\frac{2}{3}\right) = 2\left(-\frac{2}{3}\right)^3 + \frac{1}{2}\left(-\frac{2}{3}\right)^2 - 2\left(-\frac{2}{3}\right) + 9$$
$$\approx 9.96$$

Therefore, the y-coordinate of the local maximum of the function $f(x)$ is 9.96.

14. WR

Since the curve is a cubic function with a negative leading coefficient, the graph will begin in the second quadrant (for infinitely small values of x, $f(x)$ is very large), and the graph will end in the fourth quadrant (for infinitely large values of x, $f(x)$ is very small).

Step 1
Test the function to determine if it is odd or even.
Rewrite the equation when $f(-x)$.

$$f(x) = -\frac{4}{3}x^3 + 4x^2 - 3x$$
$$f(-x) = -\frac{4}{3}(-x)^3 + 4(-x)^2 - 3(-x)$$
$$f(-x) = \frac{4}{3}x^3 + 4x^2 + 3x$$

Since $f(-x) \neq f(x)$ and $f(-x) \neq -f(x)$, the function is neither odd nor even.

Step 2
Determine the coordinates of the y intercept.

$$f(x) = -\frac{4}{3}x^3 + 4x^2 - 3x$$
$$f(0) = -\frac{4}{3}(0)^3 + 4(0)^2 - 3(0)$$
$$f(0) = 0$$

The y-intercept is at $(0, 0)$.
Determine the coordinates of any x-intercepts.

$$f(x) = -\frac{4}{3}x^3 + 4x^2 - 3x$$
$$0 = -\frac{4}{3}x^3 + 4x^2 - 3x$$
$$0 = -4x^3 + 12x^2 - 9x$$
$$0 = -x(4x^2 - 12x + 9)$$
$$0 = -x(2x - 3)(2x - 3)$$

$f(x) = 0$ when $x = 0, \frac{3}{2}$. Therefore, the x-intercepts are at $(0, 0), \left(\frac{3}{2}, 0\right)$.

Step 3
Determine intervals of increase/decrease and local extrema.
Solve for x when $f'(x) = 0$.

$$f(x) = -\frac{4}{3}x^3 + 4x^2 - 3x$$
$$f'(x) = -4x^2 + 8x - 3$$
$$0 = (-2x + 1)(2x - 3)$$
$$x = \frac{1}{2}, \frac{3}{2}$$

Interval	$f'(x)$	$f(x)$
$-\infty < x < \frac{1}{2}$	$-$	Decreasing
$\frac{1}{2} < x < \frac{3}{2}$	$+$	Increasing
$\frac{3}{2} < x < \infty$	$-$	Decreasing

There is a local minimum at $\left(\frac{1}{2}, f\left(\frac{1}{2}\right)\right) = \left(\frac{1}{2}, -\frac{2}{3}\right)$ and a local maximum at $\left(\frac{3}{2}, f\left(\frac{3}{2}\right)\right) = \left(\frac{3}{2}, 0\right)$.

Step 4
Determine the point of inflection and the intervals of concavity.
Solve for x when $f''(x) = 0$.

$$f'(x) = -4x^2 + 8x - 3$$
$$f''(x) = -8x + 8$$
$$0 = -8(x - 1)$$
$$x = 1$$

The function has a point of inflection at $(1, f(1)) = \left(1, -\frac{1}{3}\right)$. Using test points in the regions $-\infty < x < 1$ and $1 < x < \infty$, the function is concave up on $-\infty < x < 1$ and concave down on $1 < x < \infty$.

Step 5
Use the characteristics identified to graph an approximate solution.

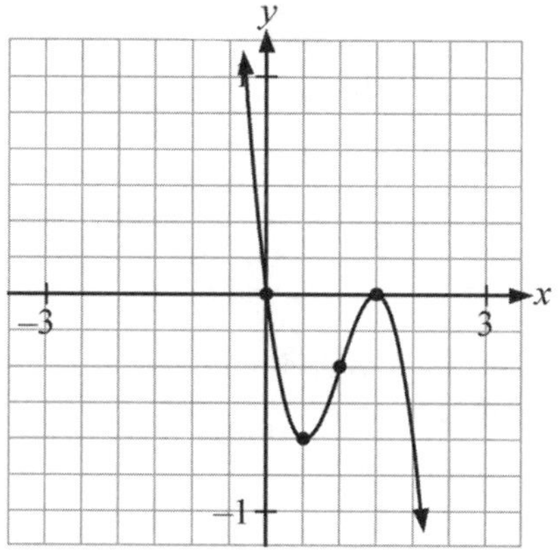

15. A

When given the position function of an object, the acceleration of the object can be found by taking the second derivative of the position function.
To determine which of the given position functions would yield a constant acceleration, find the second derivative (acceleration function) of each position function.

Determine the second derivative of $s(t) = 2t^2 - 9t + 7$.

$$s(t) = 2t^2 - 9t + 7$$
$$s'(t) = v(t) = 4t - 9$$
$$s''(t) = v'(t) = a(t) = 4$$

Determine the second derivative of $s(t) = 7t^3 - 4t^2 - 3t$.

$$s(t) = 7t^3 - 4t^2 - 3t$$
$$s'(t) = v(t) = 21t^2 - 8t - 3$$
$$s''(t) = v'(t) = a(t) = 42t - 8$$

Determine the second derivative of $s(t) = 3t^3 - 5t^2 + 4t - 1$.

$$s(t) = 3t^3 - 5t^2 + 4t - 1$$
$$s'(t) = v(t) = 9t^2 - 10t + 4$$
$$s''(t) = v'(t) = a(t) = 18t - 10$$

Determine the second derivative of $s(t) = 5t^4 - 4t^3 + 4t - 3$.

$$s(t) = 5t^4 - 4t^3 + 4t - 3$$
$$s'(t) = v(t) = 20t^3 - 12t^2 + 4$$
$$s''(t) = v'(t) = a(t) = 60t^2 - 24t$$

The function $s(t) = 2t^2 - 9t + 7$ has a second derivative with a constant value; therefore, it has a constant acceleration.

16. B

The velocity of an object is the instantaneous rate of change of the object's displacement with respect to time. In other words, the first derivative graph of a displacement-time graph is a velocity-time graph.

In this case, the velocity-time graph is made up of six polynomial elements to correspond with the six polynomial elements of the displacement-time graph. The degree of each element in the velocity-time graph will be 1 degree less than the corresponding element of the displacement-time graph.

The velocity during each stage of the graph is described as follows:

Stage 1
The displacement is constant. In other words, the rate of change of the displacement at this stage is zero. Therefore, the velocity over the same time interval will be zero.

Stage 2
The displacement is decreasing in a linear fashion. This line is a polynomial of degree 1. Therefore, the velocity over the same interval will be constant (degree 0) and negative.
The rate of change of the displacement at this stage is approximately −4. Therefore, the velocity at this stage is approximately −4.

Stage 3
The displacement is constant. In other words, the rate of change of the displacement at this stage is zero. Therefore, the velocity over the same time interval will be zero.

Stage 4
The displacement is decreasing in a linear fashion. This line is a polynomial of degree 1. Therefore, the velocity over the same interval will be constant (degree 0) and negative.

The rate of change of the displacement at this stage is approximately $-\frac{1}{2}$. Therefore, the velocity at this stage is approximately $-\frac{1}{2}$.

Stage 5
The displacement is constant. In other words, the rate of change of the displacement at this stage is zero. Therefore, the velocity over the same time interval will be zero.

Stage 6
The displacement is increasing in a linear fashion. This line is a polynomial of degree 1. Therefore, the velocity over the same interval will be constant (degree 0) and positive.

The rate of change of the displacement at this stage is approximately $\frac{4}{3}$. Therefore, the velocity at this stage is approximately $\frac{4}{3}$.

The velocity-time graph that relates to the given displacement-time graph is shown.

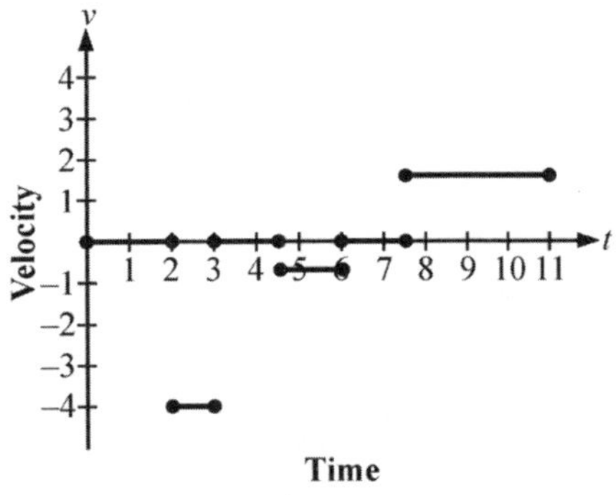

From the velocity-time graph, the magnitude of the velocity is greatest on the interval $2 < t < 3$ which corresponds to stage 2.

17. 45

Because the height function, $h(t) = -5t^2 + 30t$, has a negative a-value in a quadratic function of the form $h(t) = at^2 + bt + c$, it is a parabola that opens downward. Therefore, the function reaches a maximum (rather than a minimum).

The maximum height occurs when the rock stops travelling, just before it begins to fall toward the ground. The velocity of the rock at its maximum height is 0 m/s.

Step 1
Determine when the rock reaches its maximum height.
Find the velocity function (the first derivative of the position function), set it equal to 0, and solve for t.

$$\begin{aligned} h(t) &= -5t^2 + 30t \\ h'(t) = v(t) &= -10t + 30 \\ 0 &= -10t + 30 \\ t &= 3 \end{aligned}$$

Therefore, the rock reaches its maximum height after 3 s.

Step 2
Determine the maximum height of the rock.
To determine the maximum height reached by the rock, evaluate the height function when $t = 3$, i.e., $h(3)$.

$$\begin{aligned} h(t) &= -5t^2 + 30t \\ h(3) &= -5(3)^2 + 30(3) \\ &= -45 + 90 \\ &= 45 \end{aligned}$$

The maximum height reached by the rock is 45 m after 3 s.

18. D

The rate of change of the amount of gasoline in a fuel truck is given by $R(t) = 2\ 000e^{-0.2t}$ gal/h.

Solve for t when $R(t) = 225$.

$$\begin{aligned} 225 &= 2\ 000e^{-0.2t} \\ \frac{225}{2\ 000} &= e^{-0.2t} \\ \ln\left(\frac{225}{2\ 000}\right) &= \ln e^{-0.2t} \\ \ln\left(\frac{225}{2\ 000}\right) &= -0.2t\ln e \\ \ln\left(\frac{225}{2\ 000}\right) &= -0.2t \\ -\frac{1}{0.2}\ln\left(\frac{225}{2\ 000}\right) &= t \\ 10.9 &= t \end{aligned}$$

The rate of leakage first drops below 225 gal/h after approximately 10.9 h.

19. A

On the volume-time graph, the instantaneous rate of drainage is shown by the slope of the line tangent to the curve at any given instant within the draining period. As the curve indicates, the rate of drainage is greatest immediately after drainage begins (at the steepest part of the curve). With time, the rate slows as the volume in the tank decreases (as the curve flattens out).

Therefore, compared with the other times given, the rate of drainage at 5 min is the greatest.

20. 9882

To determine the rate of growth of the bacteria after 5 h, evaluate $g(5)$.

$$g(t) = 1\,000(2.5)^{\frac{t}{2}}$$
$$\begin{aligned} g(5) &= 1\,000(2.5)^{\frac{5}{2}} \\ &= 1\,000(2.5)^{2.5} \\ &= 9\,882 \end{aligned}$$

The growth rate is 9 882 bacteria/h.

21. B

If the electric potential of a dying battery is given by the function $P = 10 - (0.04)t^2$, then the rate of change of the battery's electric potential after 3 h can be found by evaluating the derivative of the given function at $t = 3$.

$$\begin{aligned} P &= 10 - (0.04)t^2 \\ \frac{dP}{dt} &= -(0.04)(2t) \\ &= -0.08t \\ \left.\frac{dp}{dt}\right|_{t=3} &= -0.08(3) \\ &= -0.24 \end{aligned}$$

The rate of change of the electric potential of the dying battery after 3 h is -0.24 V/h.

22. A

Step 1
The volume of a cylinder is given by the formula $V = \pi r^2 h$ in which r is the radius, and h is the height.

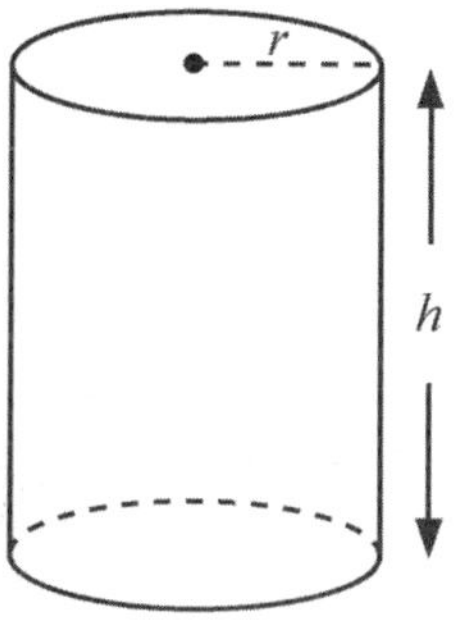

For this particular situation, it is given that the radius is 12 cm. Since the radius of a right circular cylinder is constant, the given radius may be immediately inserted into the volume function.

$$\begin{aligned} V &= \pi r^2 h \\ &= \pi(12)^2 h \\ &= 144\pi h \end{aligned}$$

Step 2
Determine the rate of change function of the height of water in the tank with respect to time.
Differentiate the volume function with respect to time.

$$\begin{aligned} V &= 144\pi h \\ \frac{dV}{dt} &= 144\pi \frac{dh}{dt} \end{aligned}$$

Step 3
Determine the rate of change of the height of water in the tank with respect to time, given that the rate of volume increase is 80 cm³/min.

Replace $\frac{dV}{dt}$ with 80 cm³/min, and solve for $\frac{dh}{dt}$.

$$\begin{aligned} \frac{dV}{dt} &= 144\pi \frac{dh}{dt} \\ 80 &= 144\pi \frac{dh}{dt} \\ \frac{80}{144\pi} &= \frac{dh}{dt} \\ 0.18 &\approx \frac{dh}{dt} \end{aligned}$$

The rate of change of water height with respect to time is approximately 0.18 cm/min.

23. 0.29

Step 1
Determine the derivative function $W'(s)$.

$$\begin{aligned} W(s) &= 55.6 - 22.1s^{0.16} \\ W'(s) &= -22.1(0.16)s^{-0.84} \\ &= -3.536s^{-0.84} \end{aligned}$$

Step 2
Determine the rate of change of the wind chill when the wind speed is 20 mi/h.
Evaluate for $W'(s)$ when $s = 20$.

$$\begin{aligned} W'(s) &= -3.536s^{-0.84} \\ W'(20) &= -3.536(20)^{-0.84} \\ &\approx -0.29 \end{aligned}$$

Therefore, the wind chill is decreasing at a rate of approximately 0.29°F/h when the wind speed is 20 mi/h.

24. D

Step 1

Write down the information that is provided, and draw a diagram to illustrate the problem.

The relationship between the lengths of wire is given by $30 = 4x + 6y$. The sum of the areas of the square and rectangle, $A = x^2 + 2y^2$, is to be a minimum.

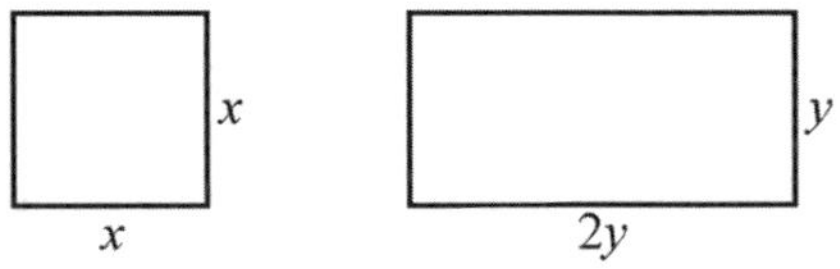

Step 2

Solve for y in terms of x using the relationship $30 = 4x + 6y$.

$$30 = 4x + 6y$$
$$30 - 4x = 6y$$
$$\frac{30 - 4x}{6} = y$$
$$5 - \frac{2}{3}x = y$$

Substitute the resulting expression for y into the area formula.

$$\begin{aligned} A &= x^2 + 2y^2 \\ &= x^2 + 2\left(5 - \frac{2}{3}x\right)^2 \\ &= x^2 + 2\left(5 - \frac{2}{3}x\right)\left(5 - \frac{2}{3}x\right) \\ &= x^2 + 2\left(25 - \frac{10}{3}x - \frac{10}{3}x + \frac{4}{9}x^2\right) \\ &= x^2 + 2\left(25 - \frac{20}{3}x + \frac{4}{9}x^2\right) \\ &= x^2 + 50 - \frac{40}{3}x + \frac{8}{9}x^2 \\ &= \frac{17}{9}x^2 - \frac{40}{3}x + 50 \end{aligned}$$

Step 3

A minimum of a function occurs when its derivative is equal to zero and the function is decreasing on the left of the zero and increasing on the right.

$$A = \frac{17}{9}x^2 - \frac{40}{3}x + 50$$
$$A' = \frac{34}{9}x - \frac{40}{3}$$
$$0 = \frac{34}{9}x - \frac{40}{3}$$
$$\frac{40}{3} = \frac{34}{9}x$$
$$\frac{360}{102} = x$$
$$\frac{60}{17} = x$$

Confirm the minimum as follows.

Interval	$A'(x)$	$A(x)$
$0 < x < \frac{60}{17}$	–	Decreasing
$\frac{60}{17} < x < \frac{30}{4}$	+	Increasing

When $x = \frac{60}{17}$, the sum of the areas is a minimum.

Step 4

Determine the value of y when $x = \frac{60}{17}$.

$$5 - \frac{2}{3}x = y$$
$$5 - \frac{2}{3}\left(\frac{60}{17}\right) = y$$
$$\frac{85}{17} - \frac{40}{17} = y$$
$$\frac{45}{17} = y$$

Step 5

Determine the length of the two wires.

Given the relationship $30 = 4x + 6y$, the two lengths of wire will be as follows.

$$\begin{aligned} 4x &= 4\left(\frac{60}{17}\right) \\ &= \frac{240}{17} \\ &\approx 14.1 \text{ m} \end{aligned}$$

$$\begin{aligned} 6y &= 6\left(\frac{45}{17}\right) \\ &= \frac{270}{17} \\ &\approx 15.9 \text{ m} \end{aligned}$$

Therefore, the longer piece of wire will be approximately 15.9 m.

25. 8

The cost function $C(x) = 4x^2 - 64x + 381$ is a quadratic function that opens upward and has a minimum value.

To determine the amount of dolls produced at minimum cost, find the first derivative, $C'(x)$, set it equal to 0, and solve for x.

$$\begin{aligned} C(x) &= 4x^2 - 64x + 381 \\ C'(x) &= 8x - 64 \\ 0 &= 8x - 64 \\ x &= 8 \end{aligned}$$

The cost is at a minimum when the number of dolls produced is 8.

26. WR

Step 1
Write an equation for the relationship between x and y.
The sum of two numbers, x and y, is 12. An equation that represents this relationship is $12 = x + y$.

Step 2
Isolate x in the sum equation.

$$\begin{aligned} 12 &= x + y \\ 12 - y &= x \end{aligned}$$

Substitute the expression for x into the product formula, $P = xy^3$.

$$\begin{aligned} P &= xy^3 \\ &= (12 - y)y^3 \\ &= 12y^3 - y^4 \end{aligned}$$

Step 3
A maximum of a function occurs where its derivative is equal to zero and the function is increasing on the left of the zero and decreasing on the right. Find the first derivative of the function, and solve for y when $P' = 0$.

$$\begin{aligned} P &= 12y^3 - y^4 \\ P' &= 36y^2 - 4y^3 \\ 0 &= 4y^2(9 - y) \\ y &= 0 \text{ or} \\ y &= 9 \end{aligned}$$

Step 4
Determine the numbers that yield the maximum product.
Since the goal is a maximum product, y cannot be zero. Thus, only consider $y = 9$.
Using the sum equation, determine the value of x when $y = 9$.

$$\begin{aligned} x &= 12 - y \\ &= 12 - 9 \\ &= 3 \end{aligned}$$

Therefore, the numbers that yield a maximum product are 3 and 9.

27. WR

To determine the height, h, of a cylinder that results in a maximum volume, the radius, r, must be written in terms of h (or vice versa) in the volume formula $V = \pi r^2 h$.

Step 1
Relate the variables h and r.
While the formula for the volume of a cylinder is given, the relationship between r and h must be established using the information that $h + C = 10$ ft, in which C is the circumference of the cylinder's base and h is the height.
Since $C = 2\pi r$,

$$\begin{aligned} h + C &= 10 \\ h + 2\pi r &= 10 \\ h &= 10 - 2\pi r \end{aligned}$$

In this case, it is easier to find h in terms of r.

Step 2
Substitute $10 - 2\pi r$ for h into the volume formula.

$$\begin{aligned} V &= \pi r^2 h \\ V &= \pi r^2(10 - 2\pi r) \\ V &= 10\pi r^2 - 2\pi^2 r^3 \end{aligned}$$

Step 3
Determine the derivative of the volume function. Set it equal to zero, and solve for r.

$$\begin{aligned} V &= 10\pi r^2 - 2\pi^2 r^3 \\ \frac{dV}{dr} &= 20\pi r - 6\pi^2 r^2 \\ 0 &= 20\pi r - 6\pi^2 r^2 \\ 0 &= 2\pi r(10 - 3\pi r) \\ r &= 0, \frac{10}{3\pi} \end{aligned}$$

Step 4
Test the validity of r.
A radius of 0 ft is not a possibility because that would result in a volume of 0 ft^3. Test only $r = \frac{10}{3\pi}$ to see if this radius yields a maximum volume.

Interval	$\frac{dV}{dr}$	V
$0 < r < \frac{10}{3\pi}$	+	Increasing
$\frac{10}{3\pi} < r < \frac{10}{2\pi}$	–	Decreasing

Therefore, the volume is a maximum when $r = \frac{10}{3\pi}$.

Step 5
Determine the height of the cylinder.
The height of a cylinder with a maximum volume is as follows:

$$\begin{aligned} h &= 10 - 2\pi r \\ &= 10 - 2\pi\left(\frac{10}{3\pi}\right) \\ &= 10 - \frac{20}{3} \\ &= \frac{10}{3} \text{ ft} \end{aligned}$$

28. A

Step 1
Using the given information, determine the exponential function that represents the number of bacteria in the culture.
The number of bacteria in the culture is given by the equation $C(t) = Ae^{kt}$.
At $t = 0$, the culture contains 1 000 bacteria.
Solve for A.

$$\begin{aligned} C(t) &= Ae^{kt} \\ C(0) &= Ae^{k(0)} \\ 1\,000 &= A \end{aligned}$$

After 4 h, the culture contains 5 000 bacteria; therefore, $C(4) = 5\,000$.
Solve for k.

$$\begin{aligned} C(t) &= Ae^{kt} \\ C(4) &= 1\,000e^{4k} \\ 5\,000 &= 1\,000e^{4k} \\ 5 &= e^{4k} \\ \ln 5 &= 4k \\ \frac{1}{4}\ln 5 &= k \end{aligned}$$

Therefore, the exponential function that represents the number of bacteria in the culture is

$C(t) = 1\,000e^{\ln 5\left(\frac{t}{4}\right)}$.

Step 2
Determine the rate of growth of the bacterial culture after 5 h.
Find the derivative function $C'(t)$, and evaluate when $t = 5$.

$$\begin{aligned} C(t) &= 1\,000e^{\ln 5\left(\frac{t}{4}\right)} \\ C'(t) &= 1\,000e^{\ln 5\left(\frac{t}{4}\right)} \cdot \left(\frac{1}{4}\right)\ln 5 \\ C'(5) &= 1\,000e^{\ln 5\left(\frac{5}{4}\right)} \cdot \left(\frac{1}{4}\right)\ln 5 \\ &\approx 3\,008 \end{aligned}$$

Therefore, the rate of growth of the bacterial culture after 5 h is 3 008 bacteria/h.

29. C

Step 1

Determine the swimmer's actual velocity.

If the swimmer swims against the current at a rate of 85 m/min, his actual velocity in the water, $V(t)$, will be the difference between his swimming rate and the velocity of the river's water flow.

$$\begin{aligned} V(t) &= 85 - v(t) \\ &= 85 - \left(32 + 5\sin\left(\sqrt{t+5}\right)\right) \\ &= 85 - 32 - 5\sin\sqrt{t+5} \\ &= 53 - 5\sin\sqrt{t+5} \end{aligned}$$

Step 2

Determine the swimmer's acceleration in the water after 10 min of swimming.

Find the derivative of the function $V(t) = 53 - 5\sin\sqrt{t+5}$, and evaluate when $t = 10$.

Make sure your calculator is in radian mode.

$$V(t) = 53 - 5\sin\sqrt{t+5}$$

$$V(t) = 53 - 5\sin(t+5)^{\frac{1}{2}}$$

$$\begin{aligned} V'(t) = a(t) &= -5\cos(t+5)^{\frac{1}{2}}\left(\frac{1}{2}\right)(t+5)^{-\frac{1}{2}} \\ &= -\frac{5}{2\sqrt{t+5}}\cos\sqrt{t+5} \end{aligned}$$

$$\begin{aligned} a(10) &= -\frac{5}{2\sqrt{10+5}}\cos\sqrt{10+5} \\ &\approx 0.48 \end{aligned}$$

After 10 min of swimming, the swimmer is accelerating in the water at a rate of approximately 0.48 m/min^2.

30. 2.87

Step 1

Determine the exponential function that represents the object's temperature after time t.

Substitute known values into the formula for Newton's law of cooling.

$$\begin{aligned} T - T_s &= (T_0 - T_s)e^{kt} \\ 750 - 35 &= (1\,500 - 35)e^{10k} \\ 715 &= 1\,465e^{10k} \end{aligned}$$

Solve for the constant, k.

$$\begin{aligned} 715 &= 1\,465e^{10k} \\ \frac{715}{1\,465} &= e^{10k} \\ \frac{143}{293} &= e^{10k} \\ \ln\left(\frac{143}{293}\right) &= 10k \\ \frac{1}{10}\ln\left(\frac{143}{293}\right) &= k \end{aligned}$$

Therefore, at time t, the object's temperature can be determined by using the following function:

$$\begin{aligned} T - 35 &= (1\,500 - 35)e^{kt} \\ T &= 1\,465e^{\ln\left(\frac{143}{293}\right)\left(\frac{t}{10}\right)} + 35 \end{aligned}$$

Step 2

Determine the time, t, when $T = 75°\text{C}$.

$$\begin{aligned} T &= 1\,465e^{\ln\left(\frac{143}{293}\right)\left(\frac{t}{10}\right)} + 35 \\ 75 &= 1\,465e^{\ln\left(\frac{143}{293}\right)\left(\frac{t}{10}\right)} + 35 \\ 40 &= 1\,465e^{\ln\left(\frac{143}{293}\right)\left(\frac{t}{10}\right)} \end{aligned}$$

$$\begin{aligned} \frac{40}{1\,465} &= e^{\ln\left(\frac{143}{293}\right)\left(\frac{t}{10}\right)} \\ \ln\left(\frac{40}{1\,465}\right) &= \ln\left(\frac{143}{293}\right)\left(\frac{t}{10}\right) \\ \frac{\ln\left(\frac{40}{1\,465}\right)}{\ln\left(\frac{143}{293}\right)} &= \frac{t}{10} \\ \frac{10\ln\left(\frac{40}{1\,465}\right)}{\ln\left(\frac{143}{293}\right)} &= t \\ 50.196\text{ min} &\approx t \end{aligned}$$

Step 3

Find the rate of change of the metal's temperature after 50.196 min.

Take the derivative of the function $T = 1\,465e^{\ln\left(\frac{143}{293}\right)\left(\frac{t}{10}\right)} + 35$, and evaluate T' when $t = 50.196$.

$$T = 1\,465e^{\ln\left(\frac{143}{293}\right)\left(\frac{t}{10}\right)} + 35$$

$$T' = 1\,465e^{\ln\left(\frac{143}{293}\right)\left(\frac{t}{10}\right)} \cdot \left(\frac{1}{10}\right)\ln\left(\frac{143}{293}\right)$$

$$\begin{aligned} &T'(50.196) \\ &= 1\,465e^{\ln\left(\frac{143}{293}\right)\left(\frac{50.196}{10}\right)} \cdot \left(\frac{1}{10}\right)\ln\left(\frac{143}{293}\right) \\ &\approx -2.87 \end{aligned}$$

The rate of temperature decrease of the metal is approximately 2.87°C/min when the temperature of the metal reaches 75°C.

Unit Test — Derivatives and their Applications

Use the following information to answer the next question.

Four pairs of graphs are shown.

1.

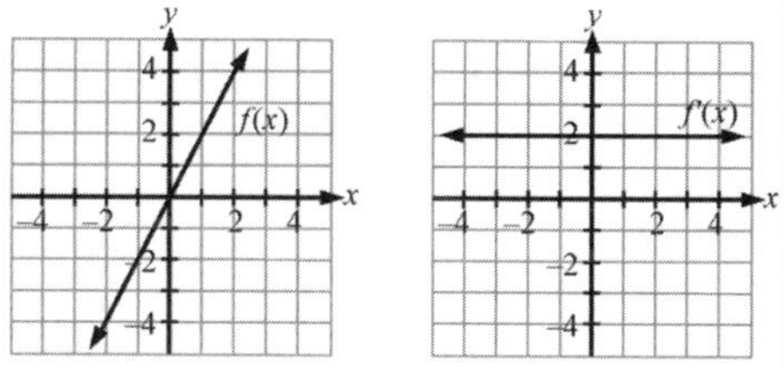

2.

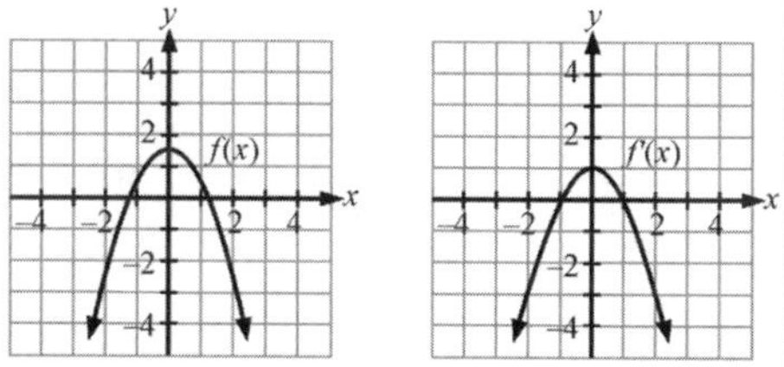

3.

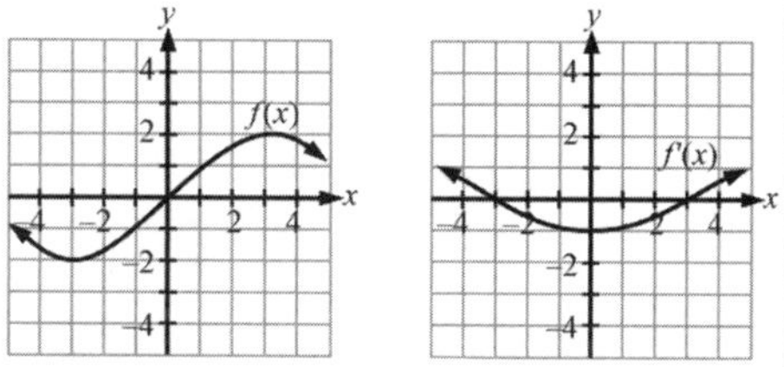

4.

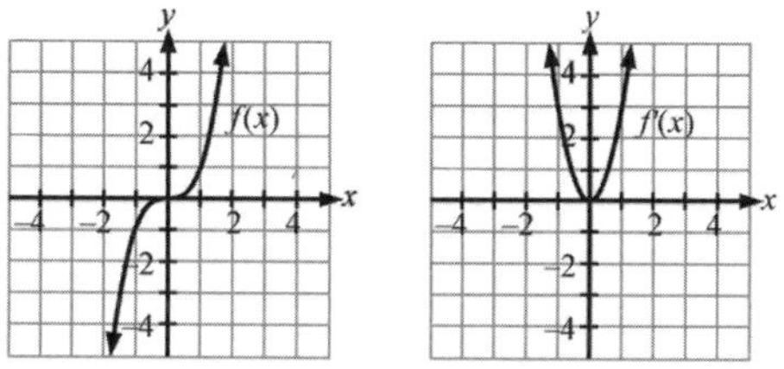

1. Which pairs of graphs represent the graph of a function and the graph of its derivative?

A. 1 and 4 **B.** 1 and 2

C. 3 and 4 **D.** 2 and 3

Use the following information to answer the next multipart question.

2. A function, $f(x)$, is cubic and has a positive leading coefficient.

Written Response

a) Describe the shape and orientation of the graph of $f'(x)$.

b) If the graph of $f(x)$ was transformed by a reflection in the x-axis to become the graph of $g(x)$, describe the differences, if any, that would be evident between the graphs of $f'(x)$ and $g'(x)$.

Use the following information to answer the next question.

The graph of a function is shown.

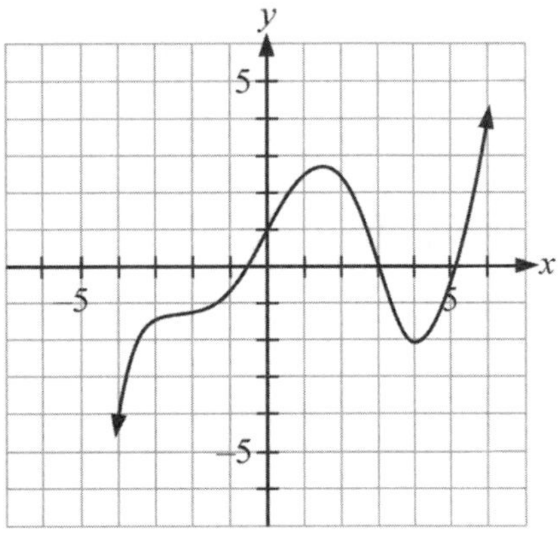

Written Response

3. Using approximate values of x, describe the concavity of the graph for all values of x.

Use the following information to answer the next question.

The graph of $f(x)$ is shown.

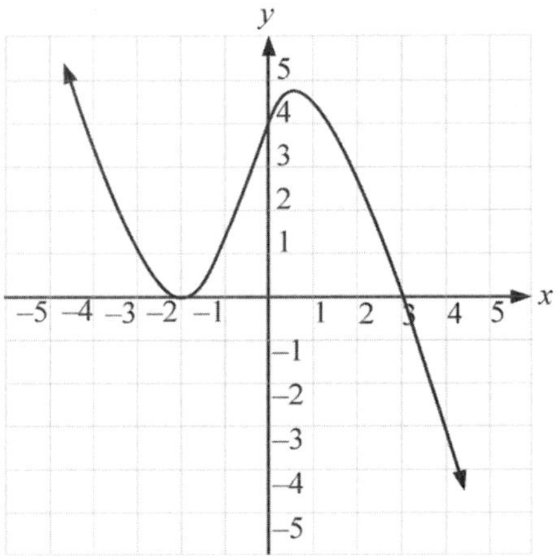

4. For which of the following approximate values of x would the graph of $f''(x)$ be equal to zero?

   A. $x = -2.3, 0.5$

   B. $x = -2.1, 3$

   C. $x = -0.6$

   D. $x = 1$

Use the following information to answer the next question.

The graph of the derivative $f'(x)$ of a smooth function $f(x)$ is shown.

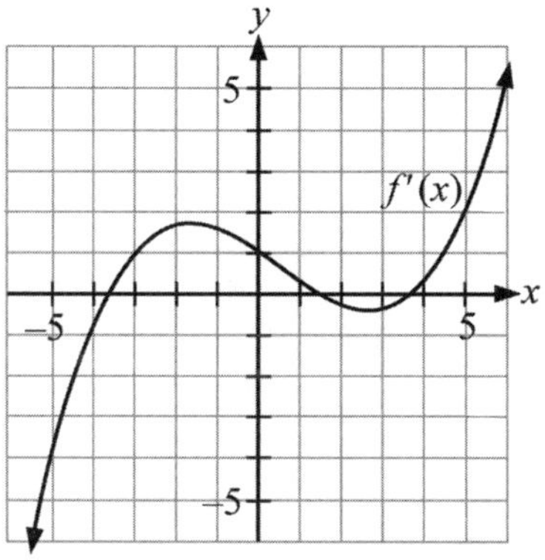

5. Which of the following shapes best describes the graph of $f''(x)$ on $-1.7 < x < 2.7$?

A. Cubic

B. Parabolic

C. Diagonal line

D. Horizontal line

Use the following information to answer the next question.

The graph of a function is shown.

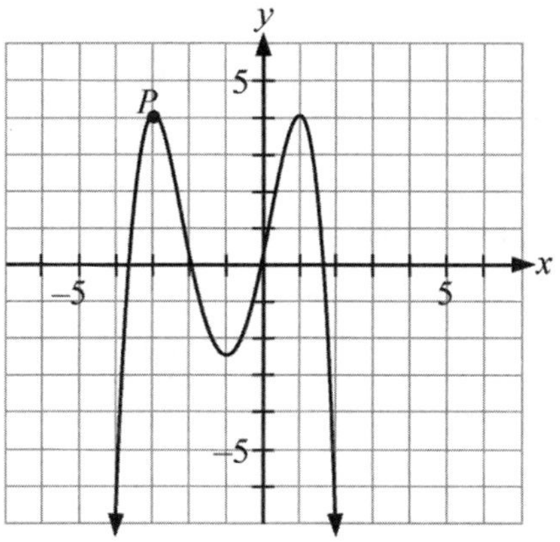

6. Which of the following pairs of relations describes characteristics of the first and second derivatives at point P labelled on the given graph?

A. $f'(x) = 0,\ f''(x) > 0$

B. $f'(x) = 0,\ f''(x) < 0$

C. $f'(x) > 0,\ f''(x) < 0$

D. $f'(x) > 0,\ f''(x) > 0$

7. On which of the following intervals is the graph of $f(x) = x^4 + 4x^3 - 18x^2 - 14x + 3$ concave up?

A. $-3 < x < 1$

B. $-3 < x < \infty$

C. $-\infty < x < 1$ and $-3 < x < \infty$

D. $-\infty < x < -3$ and $1 < x < \infty$

Use the following information to answer the next question.

A function is defined by
$f(x) = x^3 + ax^2 + bx + 1$.

Written Response

8. For what values of the constants a and b would $(1, 6)$ be a point of inflection on the graph of $f(x)$?

Written Response

9. Determine the first and second derivatives of the function $f(x) = -\frac{5}{x^3}$.

Use the following information to answer the next question.

The partial graph of a polynomial function is shown.

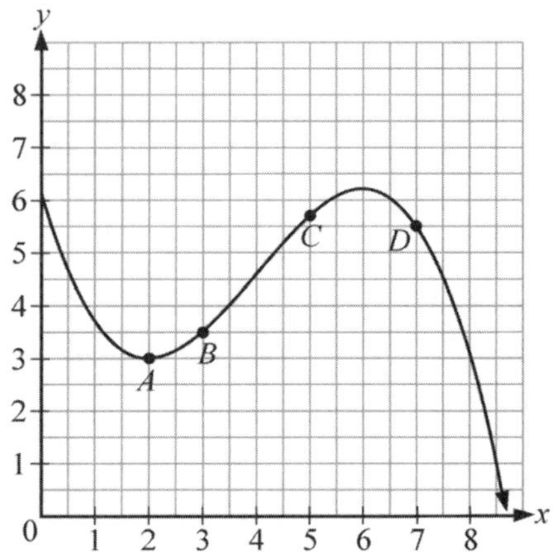

10. At which point on the graph are the first and second derivatives both positive?

A. *A* **B.** *B*

C. *C* **D.** *D*

Use the following information to answer the next question.

The graph of $f'(x)$, the derivative of a function, $f(x)$, is shown.

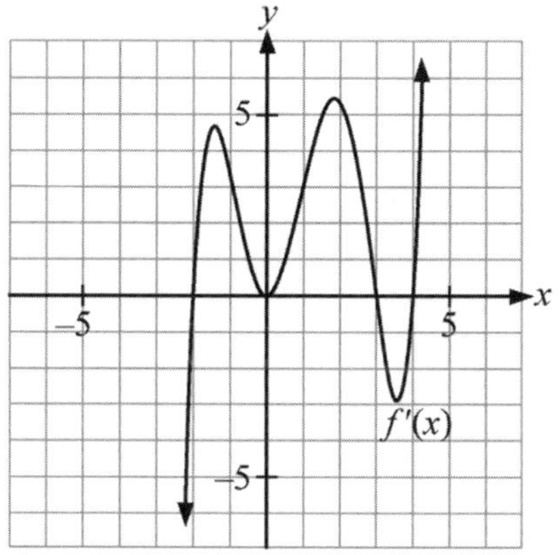

11. For approximately which of the following x-values does the graph of $f(x)$ have a local minimum?

A. $x = -2, 4$

B. $x = -2, 0$

C. $x = -3.5, 0, 4$

D. $x = -2, 0, 3, 4$

Use the following information to answer the next question.

A continuous function satisfies all of the following conditions:

A. $f(0) = f(3) = 0$,
$f(-1) = f(1) = -2$

B. $f'(-1) = f'(0) = f'(1) = 0$

C. $f'(x) < 0$ on
$-\infty < x < -1$ and $0 < x < 1$

D. $f'(x) > 0$ on
$-1 < x < 0$ and $1 < x < \infty$

E. $f''\left(-\frac{1}{2}\right) = f''\left(\frac{1}{2}\right) = f''(2) = 0$

F. $f''(x) > 0$ on
$-\infty < x < -\frac{1}{2}$ and $\frac{1}{2} < x < 2$

G. $f''(x) < 0$ on
$-\frac{1}{2} < x < \frac{1}{2}$ and $2 < x < \infty$

H. $\lim_{x \to \infty} f(x) = \infty$

I. $\lim_{x \to -\infty} f(x) = \infty$

Written Response

12. On the axes provided, sketch the graph of a continuous function that satisfies all of the given conditions.

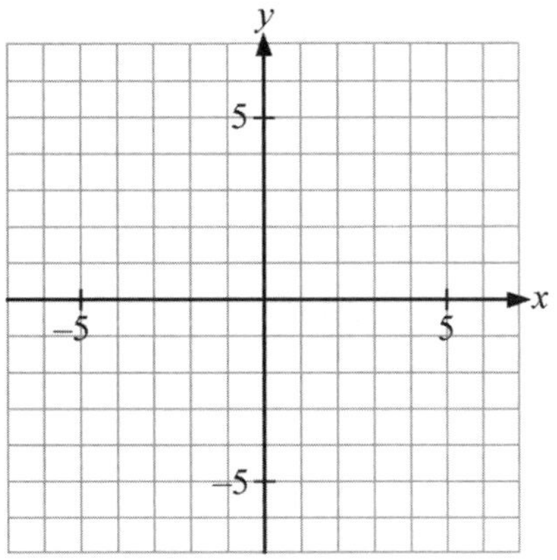

13. Which of the following steps are necessary for finding the local extrema of a polynomial function, $f(x)$?

A. Finding $f''(x)$ and solving $f(x) = f'(x)$ for x

B. Finding $f'(x)$ and solving $f(x) = f'(x)$ for x

C. Finding $f''(x)$ and solving $f''(x) = 0$ for x

D. Finding $f'(x)$ and solving $f'(x) = 0$ for x

Numerical Response

14. The y-coordinate of the point of inflection of $f(x) = x^3 - 6x^2 + 11x + 6$ is _______.

Use the following information to answer the next question.

Half the graph of an even polynomial function $f(x)$ is shown.

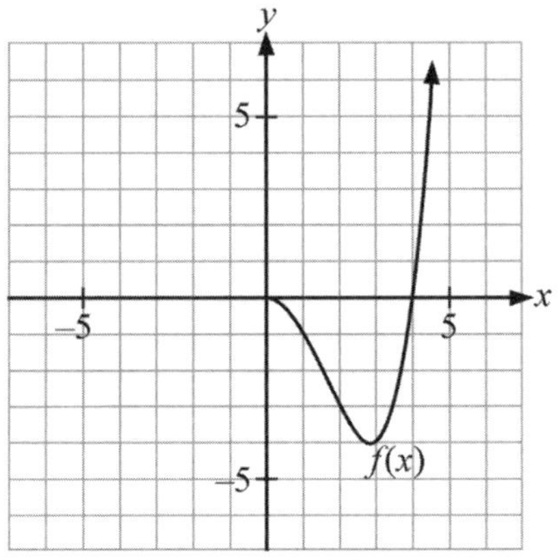

Written Response

15. Sketch the entire graph of $f(x)$ on the grid provided.

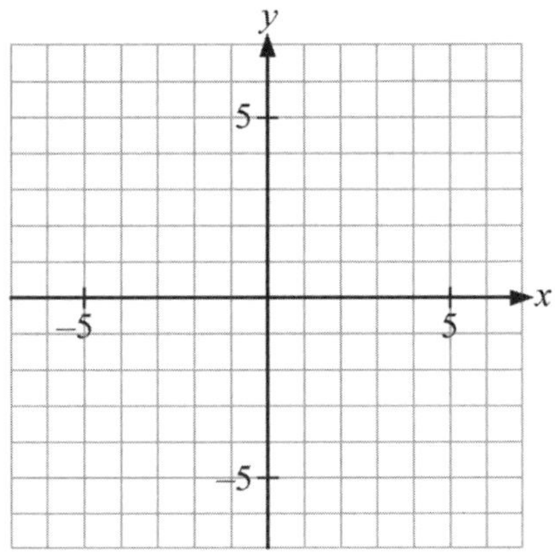

Use the following information to answer the next question.

The position function of a particle is given by $s(t) = 2t^3 - 24t^2 + 90t + 7$ for $t \geq 0$.

16. For what values of t is the velocity of the particle increasing?

A. $t > 4$ only

B. $t > 5$ only

C. $3 < t < 4$ only

D. $0 < t < 3$ and $t > 5$

Use the following information to answer the next question.

The displacement of an object is defined by the function $s(t) = 4t^3 - 9t^2 + 6t + 2$, $t \geq 0$, in which s is the displacement in metres, and t is the time in seconds.

17. What is the total distance travelled by the object in the first 4 s?

A. 126.0 m **B.** 136.5 m

C. 138.0 m **D.** 146.5 m

Use the following information to answer the next question.

The displacement-time graph of an object is shown.

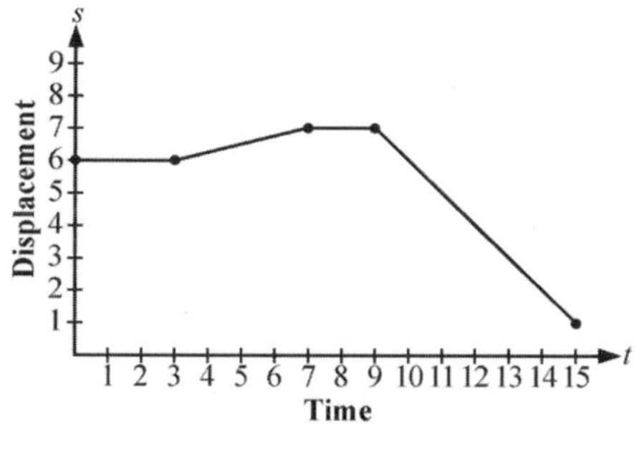

Numerical Response

18. The instantaneous acceleration of the object at 11 s appears to be ________ m/s^2.

Use the following information to answer the next question.

The power loss, P, in watts per kilometre in a particular electric conductor is given by $P = C^2r - \frac{A}{r}$, where C is the current in amps, A is a positive constant, and r is the resistance in ohms per kilometre (Ω/km).

19. For a given current, what is the resistance required for a minimum loss of power per kilometre?

A. $\frac{A}{C^2}\ \Omega/\text{km}$ **B.** $\frac{\sqrt{A}}{C}\ \Omega/\text{km}$

C. $\frac{\sqrt{C}}{A}\ \Omega/\text{km}$ **D.** $\sqrt{\frac{A}{2C}}\ \Omega/\text{km}$

Use the following information to answer the next question.

The average monthly daytime temperatures of a city in the United States over a period of six years were recorded and connected in a smooth curve as shown in the graph.

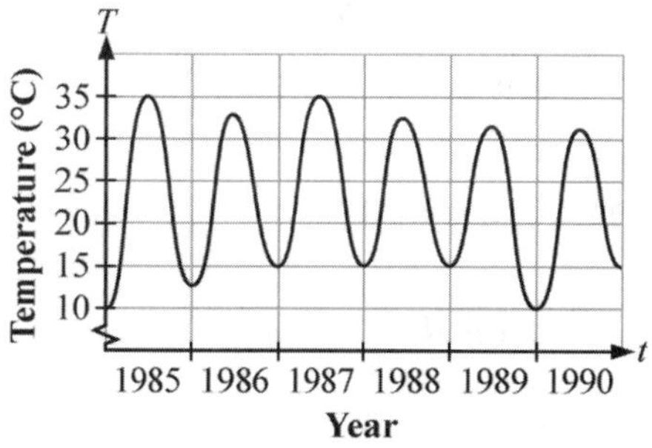

20. During which year did the average monthly temperature have the **greatest** sustained rate of increase between January and June?

A. 1985 **B.** 1986

C. 1987 **D.** 1990

Use the following information to answer the next question.

The rate of change of the height in metres of a rocket is given by the function $v(t) = 24 + 4t^2$, where t is the time in seconds after liftoff.

Numerical Response

21. The rate of change of the height of the rocket 7 s after liftoff is _________ m/s.

Use the following information to answer the next multipart question.

22. The rate at which cars pass through an intersection is known as traffic flow. The cars were counted at a busy intersection over a 30 min period of time. The function $f(t) = 6\cos\left(\frac{t}{2} - \pi\right) + 4t$, where $0 \leq t \leq 30$, models the total number of cars passing through the intersection after t minutes.

a) What was the approximate traffic flow 8 min into the monitoring period?

A. 1.73 cars/min

B. 2.27 cars/min

C. 3.32 cars/min

D. 4.12 cars/min

Written Response

b) At 8 min into the monitoring period, was the traffic flow increasing or decreasing?

Use the following information to answer the next question.

The volume of gasoline, $g(x)$, in litres used by a sport utility vehicle to travel a distance, x, in kilometres is defined by the function $g(x) = 0.06x\left(2 - e^{-\frac{x}{3}}\right)$.

23. What is the rate of gasoline consumption 250 km into a trip?

A. 0.12 L/km **B.** 3.21 L/km

C. 30.00 L/km **D.** 30.12 L/km

Use the following information to answer the next question.

A small community's water tank holds 1 500 gal of water at midnight ($t = 0$). Over the course of the next 18 h, fresh water is pumped into the tower at a rate defined by $R(t) = 85\sqrt{t}\sin\left(\frac{t}{5}\right)$, where $R(t)$ is in gal/h. Over the same 18 h, water is withdrawn from the tower such that the total amount withdrawn from the tank, in gallons, after t hours is defined by $T(t) = -520\cos\left(\frac{t}{2}\right)$.

Numerical Response

24. To the nearest tenth of an hour, how long after midnight does the water tank's volume begin to increase? _________h

Use the following information to answer the next question.

When the brightness, b, of a flashlight shone into a person's eye is increased, the eye reacts by decreasing its pupil size, P. The sensitivity, S, is defined to be the rate of change of pupil size with respect to brightness. The equation $P = \dfrac{42 + 25b^{0.3}}{1 + 4b^{0.3}}$ shows the dependence of pupil size on the brightness, in which P is measured in square millimetres, and b is measured in appropriate units of brightness.

Written Response

25. To the nearest hundredth of a square millimetre per unit of brightness, using the unsimplified equation for the sensitivity, evaluate the sensitivity for a brightness of 7 units.

Use the following information to answer the next question.

After colliding with an iceberg, a ship began to take on water at a rate defined by $R(t) = 2\,000te^{-0.2t}$, where $R(t)$ is measured in litres per hour and t is the number of hours since the collision.

26. How long after the collision was the rate of water intake at a maximum?

A. 0 h
B. 5.0 h
C. 10.0 h
D. 15.0 h

Use the following information to answer the next question.

Graham is designing a new home and wants to put in a Norman window, which is a window in the shape of a rectangle with a semicircle on top. He wants to use the 12 m of window casing he already has in storage for the perimeter of the window. The perimeter of the window is given by the equation $P = 2x + 2r + \pi r$, in which x is the height of the rectangular portion of the window in metres, and r is the radius of the semicircle in metres.

27. If area is given by the equation $A = 2xr + \dfrac{\pi r^2}{2}$, what radius will yield a window with maximum area?

A. $\dfrac{6}{4+\pi}$ m
B. $\dfrac{12}{4+\pi}$ m
C. $\dfrac{24}{4+\pi}$ m
D. $\dfrac{48}{4+\pi}$ m

Use the following information to answer the next question.

Rumours in a high school spread according to the equation $s(t) = \dfrac{1}{1 + 10e^{-0.5t}}$, where $s(t)$ is the proportion of the school's population that knows the rumour at time t in minutes.

Numerical Response

28. To the nearest tenth of a minute, the rate of spread of a rumour is a maximum after __________ min.

Use the following information to answer the next question.

The function $v(t)$ defined by $v(t) = 6 + \cos\left(\frac{t}{10}\right) + 3\sin\left(\frac{7t}{40}\right)$ is used to model the velocity of a test plane in miles per minute for $0 \le t \le 15$.

29. Rounded to the nearest hundredth, what is the acceleration of the plane after 8 min, assuming this model is valid for all flights in the test plane?

A. 0.02 mi/min^2 **B.** 0.04 mi/min^2

C. 0.32 mi/min^2 **D.** 0.34 mi/min^2

Use the following information to answer the next question.

A family driving across the United States in the summer experienced a delay when their motor home's engine overheated to 200°C. After waiting 7 min in the scorching 30°C heat, they checked the engine's temperature and discovered it had cooled to 160°C. The engine must cool to 70°C before they can resume driving.

The change in temperature of the motor home's engine follows Newton's law of cooling, represented by the exponential relationship $T - T_s = (T_0 - T_s)e^{kt}$, in which T is the object's temperature at time t, T_s is the temperature of the surroundings, T_0 is the initial temperature of the object, and k is a constant representing the relative rate of cooling of the given object.

30. If the temperature difference between the engine and the air outside changes at a rate proportional to this temperature difference, then the rate of decrease of the engine's temperature at the instant when the family can get moving again, to the nearest hundredth, is

A. 37.76°C/min

B. 2.68°C/min

C. –1.53°C/min

D. –23.15°C/min

Numerical Response

31. A small city increased in population from 45 000 to 70 000 in 35 years. Rounded to the nearest whole number, what will the rate of population increase be when the city grows to 90 000, if the population grows exponentially? ________ people/yr

Use the following information to answer the next question.

The half-life of a highly reactive substance is 6 months. The law of natural decay uses a function of the form $f(t) = Ae^{kt}$ to describe exponential decay, where $f(t)$ is the amount present after time t, A is the initial amount present, and k is a constant to be determined from given information.

Written Response

32. Use the law of natural decay to determine to the nearest tenth when the rate of decrease of mass will reach 7 kg/month if there is 84 kg initially.

Answers and Solutions — Unit Test

1. A	7. D	14. 12	21. 220	27. B
2. a) WR	8. WR	15. WR	22. a) A	28. 4.6
b) WR	9. WR	16. A	b) WR	29. A
3. WR	10. B	17. B	23. A	30. C
4. C	11. A	18. 0	24. 5.0	31. 1136
5. B	12. WR	19. B	25. WR	32. WR
6. B	13. D	20. A	26. B	

1. A

Step 1

Analyze the first pair of graphs.

In the first pair, the slope of the first graph is constant.

$$\frac{y_2 - y_1}{x_2 - x_1} = \frac{0-(-4)}{0-(-2)}$$
$$= 2$$

The graph of its derivative should be a horizontal line at $y = 2$. Therefore, the second graph is the derivative graph of the first graph.

Step 2

Analyze the second pair of graphs.

In the second pair, the first graph is a quadratic function and its derivative graph is a quadratic function. This is incorrect since the derivative graph of a quadratic function is a linear function. Therefore, the second graph is not the derivative graph of the first graph.

Step 3

Analyze the third pair of graphs.

Analyze the slope of the first graph in the third pair from left to right.

- Where $-\infty < x < -3$, the slope is negative and increasing.
- Where $x = -3$, the slope is zero.
- Where $-3 < x < 0$, the slope is positive and increasing.
- Where $0 < x < 3$, the slope is positive and decreasing.
- Where $x = 3$, the slope is zero.
- Where $3 < x < \infty$, the slope is negative and decreasing.

Graphing the slope values of $f(x)$ gives the shape of the graph of the derivative. In the second graph, the y-values start positive and decrease and then start to increase at $x = 0$. The y-values of the second graph do not correspond to the slope of the first graph. Therefore, the second graph is not the derivative graph of the first graph.

Step 4

Analyze the fourth pair of graphs.

In the fourth pair, the first graph is a cubic function and its derivative graph is a quadratic function. Inspect the points on the first graph to see that the first graph is the function $f(x) = x^3$. The derivative of $f(x)$ is $f'(x) = 3x^2$. Examine a few key points on the second graph, such as $(-1, 3)$, $(0, 0)$, and $(1, 3)$. The second graph represents $f'(x) = 3x^2$. Therefore, the second graph is the derivative graph of the first graph.

Pairs 1 and 4 represent the graph of a function and the graph of its derivative.

2. a) WR

Since the original function, $f(x)$, has a degree of 3, its derivative function, $f'(x)$, will have a degree of 2. Since $f'(x)$ has a degree of 2 and $f(x)$ has a positive leading coefficient, the graph of $f'(x)$ will be a parabola that opens upward.

b) WR

The graph of $g'(x)$ would be a reflection in the x-axis of the graph of $f'(x)$.

3. WR

The concavity of the graph for all values of x may be described as follows:

- On $x < -2$, the graph of the function is concave down.
- At $x = -2$, there is a point of inflection.
- On $-2 < x < 0$, the graph of the function is concave up.
- At $x = 0$, there is a point of inflection.
- On $0 < x < 3$, the graph of the function is concave down.
- At $x = 3$, there is a point of inflection.
- On $x > 3$, the graph of the function is concave up.

4. C

When the graph of $f''(x)$ is equal to zero, there is a point of inflection on the graph of $f(x)$. At $x = -0.6$ on the graph of $f(x)$, there is a point of inflection.

Therefore, the graph of $f''(x)$ is equal to zero at $x = -0.6$.

5. B

Using approximate x values, analyze the slope of the derivative graph on the interval $-1.7 < x < 2.7$ when it is viewed from left to right.

- $x = -1.7$, slope is zero
- $-1.7 < x < 0.8$, slope negative and decreasing
- $0.8 < x < 2.7$, slope is negative and increasing
- $x = 2.7$, slope is zero

When the approximate slope values are graphed, the result is the following:

- $x = -1.7$, there is an x intercept
- $-1.7 < x < 0.8$, y values are negative and decreasing
- $x = 0.8$, there is a local minimum
- $0.8 < x < 2.7$, y values are negative and increasing
- $x = 2.7$, there is an x intercept

Therefore, the result is a parabolic shape with a local minimum. Also, since the first derivative graph represents a cubic function, the second derivative graph should represent a quadratic function.

6. B

Point P on the graph of the function is a local maximum where the slope is zero. Therefore, the first derivative graph will be equal to zero at $x = P$. In other words, at point P on the first derivative graph, $f'(x) = 0$.

At point P on the graph of the function, the graph is concave down and decreasing. Therefore, the second derivative graph will be negative at $x = P$. In other words, at point P on the second derivative graph, $f''(x) < 0$.

7. D

Step 1
Determine the first derivative of the function $f(x)$.

$f(x) = x^4 + 4x^3 - 18x^2 - 14x + 3$
$f'(x) = 4x^3 + 12x^2 - 36x - 14$

Step 2
Determine the second derivative of the function $f(x)$.

$f'(x) = 4x^3 + 12x^2 - 36x - 14$
$f''(x) = 12x^2 + 24x - 36$

Step 3
Find the inflection points.
The points of inflection occur at the points where the second derivative is equal to 0.

$$\begin{aligned} f''(x) &= 12x^2 + 24x - 36 \\ 0 &= 12x^2 + 24x - 36 \\ &= 12(x^2 + 2x - 3) \\ &= 12(x-1)(x+3) \end{aligned}$$

Therefore, the inflection points occur at $x = 1$ and $x = -3$.

Step 4
Identify the intervals of concavity.
The function is concave down where the second derivative is negative and concave up where it is positive.

Interval	$f''(x)$	Positive / Negative
$-\infty < x < -3$	$f''(-4) = 60$	Positive
$-3 < x < 1$	$f''(0) = -36$	Negative
$1 < x < \infty$	$f''(2) = 60$	Positive

Therefore, the function is concave up on the intervals $-\infty < x < -3$ and $1 < x < \infty$.

8. WR

The points of inflection occur at values of x when $f''(x) = 0$.

Step 1
Determine the second derivative of $f(x)$.

$f(x) = x^3 + ax^2 + bx + 1$
$f'(x) = 3x^2 + 2ax + b$
$f''(x) = 6x + 2a$

Step 2
Determine the value of a.
Since $(1, 6)$ is a point of inflection on the graph of $f(x)$, then $f''(1) = 0$.
If $f''(1) = 0$, substitute into the second derivative equation, and solve for a.

$$\begin{aligned} f''(x) &= 6x + 2a \\ f''(1) &= 6 + 2a \\ 0 &= 6 + 2a \\ a &= -3 \end{aligned}$$

Step 3
Determine the value of b.
Since the constant b is not part of the second derivative, its value can be determined by substituting the value of $a = -3$ and the coordinates of the point (1, 6) into the original function $f(x) = x^3 + ax^2 + bx + 1$.

$$f(x) = x^3 + ax^2 + bx + 1$$
$$6 = (1)^3 + (-3)(1)^2 + b(1) + 1$$
$$6 = 1 - 3 + b + 1$$
$$7 = b$$

Therefore, the constants are $a = -3$ and $b = 7$.

9. WR

Step 1
Determine the first derivative of the function.

$$f(x) = -\frac{5}{x^3}$$
$$f(x) = -5x^{-3}$$
$$f'(x) = 15x^{-4}$$
$$f'(x) = \frac{15}{x^4}$$

Step 2
Determine the second derivative of the function.

$$f'(x) = \frac{15}{x^4}$$
$$f'(x) = 15x^{-4}$$
$$f''(x) = -60x^{-5}$$
$$f''(x) = -\frac{60}{x^5}$$

10. B

The first derivative graph will be positive at points on the original function where the slope is positive. The second derivative graph will be positive at points on the original function where concavity is positive.

The first derivative is positive at point B because the slope is positive. The second derivative is positive at point B because the concavity is also positive.

Points A and D are not positive on the first derivative graph because slope is zero at point A and slope is negative at point D. The first derivative is positive at point C because the slope is positive. However, the second derivative is negative at point C because the concavity is negative.

11. A

Step 1
Determine x-values of the local maxima/minima.
The points of local maxima/minima occur when the first derivative is equal to 0.
The first derivative graph is equal to zero at $x = -2, 0, 3,$ and 4. There is a local maximum or local minimum at these points.

Step 2
Find the x-value(s) of the local minima.
At a local minimum point, the derivative is negative to the left and positive to the immediate right of the point.
From the derivative graph $f'(x)$, the derivative is negative to the left and positive to the immediate right of the point at $x = -2$ and $x = 4$.
Therefore, there is a local minimum at $x = -2$ and $x = 4$.

12. WR

The function graph has the following characteristics:

A. Passes through the points (0, 0), (3, 0), (−1, −2), and (1, −2).
B. There are local extrema at (−1, −2), (0, 0), and (1, −2).
C. Decreasing on the intervals $-\infty < x < -1$ and $0 < x < 1$.
D. Increasing on the intervals $-1 < x < 0$ and $1 < x < \infty$.
E. There are points of inflection at $x = -\frac{1}{2}, \frac{1}{2}$, and 2.
F. Concave up on the intervals $-\infty < x < -\frac{1}{2}$ and $\frac{1}{2} < x < 2$.
G. Concave down on the intervals $-\frac{1}{2} < x < \frac{1}{2}$ and $2 < x < \infty$.
H. As x approaches infinity, y approaches infinity.
I. As x approaches negative infinity, y approaches infinity.

Using the characteristics listed, sketch the graph of the function.

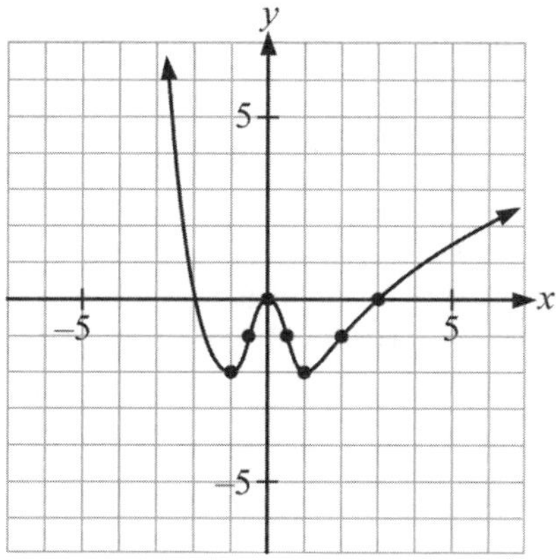

13. D

The local extrema of a polynomial function, $f(x)$, occurs when the first derivative (slope) of the function is equal to zero. Therefore, necessary steps involved in finding the local extrema of $f(x)$ include finding the derivative function, $f'(x)$, and solving $f'(x) = 0$ for x.

14. 12

Step 1
Determine the second derivative function of $f(x)$.

$f(x) = x^3 - 6x^2 + 11x + 6$
$f'(x) = 3x^2 - 12x + 11$
$f''(x) = 6x - 12$

Step 2
Determine the x-coordinate of the point of inflection. The inflection point occurs when the second derivative, $f''(x)$, is equal to zero.
Solve for x when $f''(x) = 0$.

$f''(x) = 6x - 12$
$0 = 6x - 12$
$12 = 6x$
$x = 2$

Therefore, there is an inflection point at $x = 2$.

Step 3
Determine the y-coordinate of the point of inflection.
Solve for $f(x)$ when $x = 2$.

$f(x) = x^3 - 6x^2 + 11x + 6$
$f(2) = 2^3 - 6(2)^2 + 11(2) + 6$
$= 8 - 24 + 22 + 6$
$= 12$

The y-coordinate of the point of inflection is 12.

15. WR

When a polynomial is even, the graph of the polynomial is symmetrical about the y-axis. Reflect the half of graph $f(x)$ about the y-axis to obtain the other half.

Step 1
Choose key points on the half graph of $f(x)$, and multiply the x-coordinates by -1 to obtain a new set of points.

$(4.5, 5) \rightarrow (-4.5, 5)$
$(4, 0) \rightarrow (-4, 0)$
$(2.9, -4) \rightarrow (-2.9, -4)$
$(2, -3) \rightarrow (-2, -3)$
$(1, -1) \rightarrow (-1, -1)$
$(0, 0) \rightarrow (0, 0)$

Step 2
Graph the new points, and connect the points using a smooth curve.

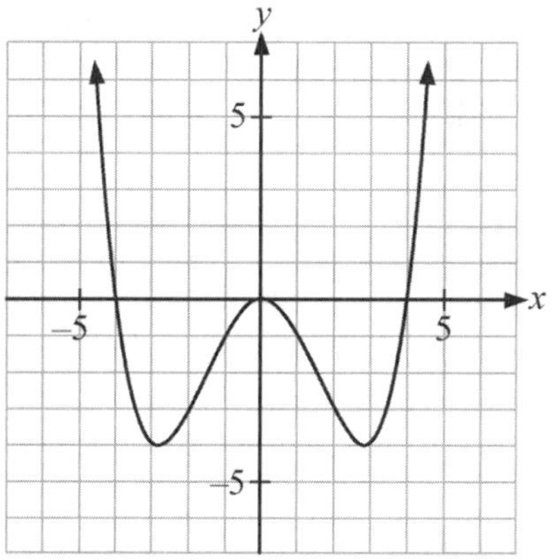

16. A

Step 1
Determine the second derivative of $s(t)$ to get the acceleration function $a(t)$.

$s(t) = 2t^3 - 24t^2 + 90t + 7$
$s'(t) = v(t) = 6t^2 - 48t + 90$
$s''(t) = v'(t) = a(t) = 12t - 48$

Step 2
Determine when acceleration is zero.
Calculate t when $a(t) = 0$.

$a(t) = 12t - 48$
$0 = 12t - 48$
$t = 4$

Step 3
The velocity of a particle is increasing when the acceleration of the particle is positive.
Use a test point on the interval $0 < t < 4$ to determine when $v(t)$ is increasing or decreasing.
Solve $a(t)$ when $t = 1$.

$$a(t) = 12t - 48$$
$$a(1) = 12(1) - 48$$
$$= -36$$

Acceleration is negative; therefore, the velocity of the particle is decreasing on the time interval $0 < t < 4$.

Step 4
Use a test point on the interval $4 < t < \infty$ to determine when $v(t)$ is increasing or decreasing.
Solve $a(t)$ when $t = 5$.

$$a(t) = 12t - 48$$
$$a(5) = 12(5) - 48$$
$$= 12$$

Acceleration is positive; therefore, the velocity of the particle is increasing on the time interval $4 < t < \infty$ (i.e.,$t > 4$) only.

17. B

Step 1
Find the first derivative of the displacement function to get the velocity function.

$$s(t) = 4t^3 - 9t^2 + 6t + 2$$
$$s'(t) = v(t) = 12t^2 - 18t + 6$$

Step 2
Find when the velocity of the object is zero. That is, determine when the object stops and possibly changes direction.
Determine the value or values of t when $v(t) = 0$.

$$v(t) = 12t^2 - 18t + 6$$
$$0 = 6(2t^2 - 3t + 1)$$
$$0 = 6(2t^2 - 2t - 1t + 1)$$
$$0 = 6(2t(t-1) - 1(t-1))$$
$$0 = 6(t-1)(2t-1)$$
$$t = 1, t = \frac{1}{2}$$

Step 3
Calculate the total distance travelled by the object.
The object is in motion over the following time intervals:

$$0 < t < \frac{1}{2}$$
$$\frac{1}{2} < t < 1$$
$$1 < t < 4$$

Take the sum of the distance travelled in each time interval to find the total distance travelled. Disregard the direction of travel in each time interval.
The total distance travelled is calculated as follows:

$$= \left(\begin{array}{l}[s(4) - s(1)] + \left[s(1) - s\left(\frac{1}{2}\right)\right] \\ + \left[s\left(\frac{1}{2}\right) - s(0)\right]\end{array}\right)$$
$$= \left(\begin{array}{l}[138 - 3] + [3 - 3.25] \\ + [3.25 - 2]\end{array}\right)$$
$$= 135 + 0.25 + 1.25$$
$$= 136.5 \text{ m}$$

18. 0

At $t = 11$ s, the slope of the displacement-time graph is decreasing in a linear fashion, which means that the velocity at that same time would be a negative constant. Therefore, the acceleration at $t = 11$ s would be 0 m/s^2.

19. B

Step 1
Find the derivative of the power loss function, $P = C^2 r + \frac{A}{r}$, with respect to r.

$$P = C^2 r + \frac{A}{r}$$
$$P = C^2 r + Ar^{-1}$$
$$\frac{dP}{dr} = C^2 - Ar^{-2}$$

Step 2

Solve for r when $\frac{dP}{dr} = 0$.

$$\frac{dP}{dr} = C^2 - Ar^{-2}$$
$$0 = C^2 - \frac{A}{r^2}$$
$$\frac{A}{r^2} = C^2$$
$$\frac{A}{C^2} = r^2$$
$$\sqrt{\frac{A}{C^2}} = r$$
$$\frac{\sqrt{A}}{C} = r$$

The resistance required for a minimum loss of power per kilometre is $\frac{\sqrt{A}}{C}$ Ω/km.

20. A

In 1985, the average monthly daytime temperature for the first part of the year increased the most.

The average temperature in January 1985 started at the lowest recorded value of the given six years and, by June, had reached the highest recorded value of the given years. This resulted in the greatest six-month rate of increase.

21. 220

Since the rate of change function for the height of the rocket is given, evaluate the rate of change function (velocity function) for $t = 7$.

$$v(t) = 24 + 4t^2$$
$$\begin{aligned} v(7) &= 24 + 4(7)^2 \\ &= 24 + 196 \\ &= 220 \end{aligned}$$

The rate of change of the height of the rocket 7 s after liftoff is 220 m/s.

22. a) A

Step 1

Determine the first derivative of $f(t)$.

$$f(t) = 6\cos\left(\frac{t}{2} - \pi\right) + 4t$$
$$f'(t) = -6\sin\left(\frac{t}{2} - \pi\right)\left(\frac{1}{2}\right) + 4$$
$$f'(t) = -3\sin\left(\frac{t}{2} - \pi\right) + 4$$

The derivative, $f'(t)$, models the rate of change of the number of cars (traffic flow) passing through the intersection at some time, t.

Step 2

Solve $f'(8)$ when $t = 8$. Remember to make sure the calculator is in radian mode.

$$f'(t) = -3\sin\left(\frac{t}{2} - \pi\right) + 4$$
$$f'(8) = -3\sin\left(\frac{8}{2} - \pi\right) + 4$$
$$f'(8) \approx 1.73$$

Therefore, at 8 min into the monitoring period, the traffic flow was 1.73 cars/min.

b) WR

Step 1

Determine the function that represents the rate of change of traffic flow.

Find the second derivative of $f(t)$.

$$f(t) = 6\cos\left(\frac{t}{2} - \pi\right) + 4t$$
$$f'(t) = -3\sin\left(\frac{t}{2} - \pi\right) + 4$$
$$\begin{aligned} f''(t) &= -3\cos\left(\frac{t}{2} - \pi\right)\left(\frac{1}{2}\right) \\ &= -\frac{3}{2}\cos\left(\frac{t}{2} - \pi\right) \end{aligned}$$

Step 2

Using the second derivative function, determine if traffic flow was increasing or decreasing 8 min into the monitoring period.

Solve $f''(t)$ when $t = 8$.

$$f''(t) = -\frac{3}{2}\cos\left(\frac{t}{2} - \pi\right)$$
$$\begin{aligned} f''(8) &= -\frac{3}{2}\cos\left(\frac{8}{2} - \pi\right) \\ &\approx -0.98 \end{aligned}$$

Since the rate of change of the traffic flow is negative, the traffic flow was decreasing 8 min after monitoring.

23. A

Step 1

Determine the function that represents the rate of gas consumption.

Find the first derivative function of $g(x)$.

$$g(x) = 0.06x\left(2 - e^{-\frac{x}{3}}\right)$$
$$\begin{aligned} g'(x) &= \begin{pmatrix} 0.06x\left(-e^{-\frac{x}{3}}\right)\left(-\frac{1}{3}\right) \\ +\left(2 - e^{-\frac{x}{3}}\right)(0.06) \end{pmatrix} \\ &= 0.02xe^{-\frac{x}{3}} + 0.12 - 0.06e^{-\frac{x}{3}} \end{aligned}$$

Step 2
Determine the rate of gas consumption 250 km into a trip.
Solve for $g'(250)$.

$$g'(x) = \left(\begin{matrix} 0.02xe^{-\frac{x}{3}} + 0.12 \\ - 0.06e^{-\frac{x}{3}} \end{matrix}\right)$$

$$g'(250) = \left(\begin{matrix} 0.02(250)e^{-\frac{250}{3}} + 0.12 \\ - 0.06e^{-\frac{250}{3}} \end{matrix}\right)$$
$$= 0.12$$

The rate of gasoline consumption 250 km into a trip is 0.12 L/km.

24. 5.0

Step 1
Determine the function that represents the rate at which water is withdrawn from the water tank.
Find the first derivative of the function
$T(t) = -520\cos\left(\frac{t}{2}\right)$.

$$T(t) = -520\cos\left(\frac{t}{2}\right)$$
$$T'(t) = 520\sin\left(\frac{t}{2}\right) \cdot \left(\frac{1}{2}\right)$$
$$= 260\sin\left(\frac{t}{2}\right)$$

Step 2
Determine the function that represents the rate at which the amount of water in the water tank is changing.
The rate at which the amount of water in the tank is changing, C, can be determined from the difference between the rate at which fresh water is being pumped into the tank, $R(t)$, and the rate at which water is being withdrawn, $T'(t)$.

$$C(t) = R(t) - T'(t)$$
$$= 85\sqrt{t}\sin\left(\frac{t}{5}\right) - 260\sin\left(\frac{t}{2}\right)$$

Step 3
Determine how long after midnight the water tank's volume begins to increase.
Graph the rate of change function
$C(t) = 85\sqrt{t}\sin\left(\frac{t}{5}\right) - 260\sin\left(\frac{t}{2}\right)$, and determine at what time, t, it first becomes positive; this will correspond to the time at which the overall volume in the tank starts increasing.
Using a graphing calculator, enter
$Y_1 = 85\sqrt{(X)}\sin(X/5) - 260\sin(X/2)$ in the [Y =] window. Then, press [WINDOW], enter x:[0, 18, 2] and y:[−1 000, 1 000, 200], and press [GRAPH].

Press [2nd] [TRACE] and select 2:zero to determine that the rate of change of the water volume is 0 when $x = t \approx 4.969$. Immediately after this time, the rate of change of water volume is positive and increasing. Therefore, the volume in the tank begins increasing 5.0 h after midnight.

25. WR

Step 1
Determine the function that represents sensitivity, S.
Since sensitivity, S, is the rate of change of pupil size, P, with respect to brightness, b, an equation for the sensitivity can be found by differentiating the given function, P, with respect to b.

$$P = \left(42 + 25b^{0.3}\right)\left(1 + 4b^{0.3}\right)^{-1}$$
$$\frac{dP}{db} = S$$
$$= \left(\begin{matrix} \left(42 + 25b^{0.3}\right) \\ \times\ (-1)\left(1 + 4b^{0.3}\right)^{-2}\left(1.2b^{-0.7}\right) \\ +\ \left(1 + 4b^{0.3}\right)^{-1}\left(7.5b^{-0.7}\right) \end{matrix}\right)$$

Step 2
Determine the sensitivity for a brightness of 7 units.
Calculate S when $b = 7$.

$$S = \left(\begin{matrix} \left(42 + 25b^{0.3}\right) \\ \times\ (-1)\left(1 + 4b^{0.3}\right)^{-2}\left(1.2b^{-0.7}\right) \\ +\ \left(1 + 4b^{0.3}\right)^{-1}\left(7.5b^{-0.7}\right) \end{matrix}\right)$$

$$S(7) = \left(\begin{matrix} \left(42 + 25(7)^{0.3}\right) \\ \times\ (-1)\left(1 + 4(7)^{0.3}\right)^{-2} \times 1.2(7)^{-0.7} \\ +\ \left(1 + 4(7)^{0.3}\right)^{-1}\left(7.5(7)^{-0.7}\right) \end{matrix}\right)$$
$$\approx -0.16$$

Therefore, the sensitivity for a brightness of 7 units is approximately −0.16 mm^2/unit of brightness.

26. B

Step 1
Find the derivative of the given function *R(t)*.

$$R(t) = 2\,000te^{-0.2t}$$
$$R'(t) = 2\,000t\left(e^{-0.2t}\right)(-0.2) + \left(e^{-0.2t}\right)(2\,000)$$
$$= 2\,000e^{-0.2t}(-0.2t + 1)$$

Step 2
Determine how long it will take for the water intake to reach a maximum.
Set $R'(t) = 0$, and solve for t.

$$R'(t) = 2\,000e^{-0.2t}(-0.2t + 1)$$
$$0 = 2\,000e^{-0.2t}(-0.2t + 1)$$
$$0 = e^{-0.2t} \text{ or } 0 = -0.2t + 1$$

Since the expression $e^{-0.2t}$ will never equal 0 (it will always be positive), there is only one value of t to consider.

$$-0.2t + 1 = 0$$
$$-0.2t = -1$$
$$t = 5$$

Step 3
Confirm the existence of a maximum at $t = 5$.

Interval	$R'(t)$	$R(t)$
$0 < t < 5$	+	Increasing
$5 < t < \infty$	–	Decreasing

The ship's water intake was at a maximum 5 h after the collision.

27. B

Draw a diagram of the window.

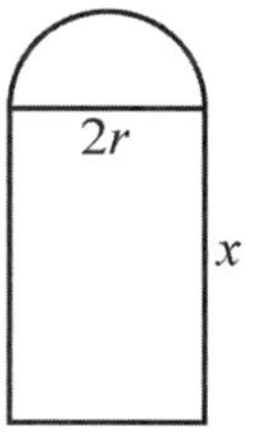

It is given that the perimeter of the window is $P = 2x + 2r + \pi r$. Since there is 12 m of window casing available,
$12 = 2x + 2r + \pi r$.

Isolate x in the perimeter equation.

$$12 = 2x + 2r + \pi r$$
$$12 - 2r - \pi r = 2x$$
$$\frac{12 - 2r - \pi r}{2} = x$$

Substitute the expression of x into the area formula.

$$A = 2xr + \frac{\pi r^2}{2}$$
$$= 2\left(\frac{12 - 2r - \pi r}{2}\right)r + \frac{\pi r^2}{2}$$
$$= 12r - 2r^2 - \pi r^2 + \frac{\pi}{2}r^2$$
$$= 12r - 2r^2 - \frac{\pi}{2}r^2$$

A maximum of a function occurs when its derivative is equal to zero and the function is increasing on the left and decreasing on the right of the zero.

Determine the derivative function of A, and solve for x when $A' = 0$.

$$A = 12r - 2r^2 - \frac{\pi}{2}r^2$$
$$A' = 12 - 4r - \pi r$$
$$0 = 12 - 4r - \pi r$$
$$4r + \pi r = 12$$
$$r(4 + \pi) = 12$$
$$r = \frac{12}{(4 + \pi)}$$

Confirm the maximum as follows:

Interval	A'	A
$0 < x < \frac{12}{(4+\pi)}$	Positive	Increasing
$\frac{12}{(4+\pi)} < x < \frac{24}{(4+\pi)}$	Negative	Decreasing

When the radius, r, is $\frac{12}{(4+\pi)}$ m, the area of the window will be at a maximum.

28. 4.6

Step 1
Determine the first derivative $s'(t)$ of the function $s(t)$.

$$s(t) = \frac{1}{1 + 10e^{-0.5t}}$$
$$= \left(1 + 10e^{-0.5t}\right)^{-1}$$
$$s'(t) = -1\left(1 + 10e^{-0.5t}\right)^{-2}\left(10e^{-0.5t}\right)(-0.5)$$
$$= \frac{5e^{-0.5t}}{\left(1 + 10e^{-0.5t}\right)^2}$$

Step 2
Use technology to find the location of the derivative function's maximum.

Using a graphing calculator, press [Y =] and enter Y_1 = 5e^(–0.5X)/(1 + 10e^(–0.5X))^2.

Then, press [WINDOW], and enter x:[–10, 10, 1], y:[–0.5, 0.5, 0.1].
To find the maximum value of the derivative function, press [2nd] [TRACE], and select 4:maximum. Move the cursor to just left of the maximum, and press [ENTER]. Then, move the cursor to just right of the maximum, and press [ENTER] twice. The maximum occurs at approximately (4.6, 0.125).
Therefore, the rate of spread of a rumour is at a maximum after 4.6 min.

29. A

Since the function representing the velocity of the airplane is given, the function representing its acceleration can be determined.

Step 1
Find the derivative of the velocity function.

$$v(t) = 6 + \cos\left(\frac{t}{10}\right) + 3\sin\left(\frac{7t}{40}\right)$$
$$v'(t) = a(t)$$
$$= -\sin\left(\frac{t}{10}\right)\left(\frac{1}{10}\right) + 3\cos\left(\frac{7t}{40}\right)\left(\frac{7}{40}\right)$$
$$= -\frac{1}{10}\sin\left(\frac{t}{10}\right) + \frac{21}{40}\cos\left(\frac{7t}{40}\right)$$

Step 2
Determine the acceleration of the plane after 8 min.
Calculate the acceleration function for $t = 8$.
Remember to make sure the calculator is in radian mode.

$$a(t) = -\frac{1}{10}\sin\left(\frac{t}{10}\right) + \frac{21}{40}\cos\left(\frac{7t}{40}\right)$$
$$a(8) = -\frac{1}{10}\sin\left(\frac{8}{10}\right) + \frac{21}{40}\cos\left(\frac{7(8)}{40}\right)$$
$$\approx 0.02$$

Rounded to the nearest hundredth, the acceleration of the plane after 8 min is 0.02 mi/min^2.

30. C

Step 1
Determine the exponential function that represents the motor home's engine temperature after time t.
Substitute known values into the formula for Newton's law of cooling.

$$T - T_s = (T_0 - T_s)e^{kt}$$
$$160 - 30 = (200 - 30)e^{7k}$$
$$130 = 170e^{7k}$$

Solve for the constant, k.

$$130 = 170e^{7k}$$
$$\frac{130}{170} = e^{7k}$$
$$\ln\left(\frac{13}{17}\right) = 7k$$
$$\frac{1}{7}\ln\left(\frac{13}{17}\right) = k$$

Therefore, at time t, the engine's temperature can be determined as follows:

$$T - 30 = (200 - 30)e^{kt}$$
$$T = 170e^{\ln\left(\frac{13}{17}\right)\left(\frac{t}{7}\right)} + 30$$

Step 2
Determine the time, t, when $T = 70°C$.

$$T = 170e^{\ln\left(\frac{13}{17}\right)\left(\frac{t}{7}\right)} + 30$$
$$70 = 170e^{\ln\left(\frac{13}{17}\right)\left(\frac{t}{7}\right)} + 30$$
$$40 = 170e^{\ln\left(\frac{13}{17}\right)\left(\frac{t}{7}\right)}$$
$$\frac{4}{17} = e^{\ln\left(\frac{13}{17}\right)\left(\frac{t}{7}\right)}$$
$$\ln\left(\frac{4}{17}\right) = \ln\left(\frac{13}{17}\right)\left(\frac{t}{7}\right)$$
$$\frac{\ln\left(\frac{4}{17}\right)}{\ln\left(\frac{13}{17}\right)} = \frac{t}{7}$$
$$\frac{7\ln\left(\frac{4}{17}\right)}{\ln\left(\frac{13}{17}\right)} = t$$
$$37.755 \approx t$$

Step 3

Find the rate of change of the motor home's engine temperature at $t = 37.755$.

Take the derivative of the function

$T = 170e^{\ln\left(\frac{13}{17}\right)\left(\frac{t}{7}\right)} + 30$, and evaluate T' when $t = 37.755$.

$$T = 170e^{\ln\left(\frac{13}{17}\right)\left(\frac{t}{7}\right)} + 30$$

$$T' = 170e^{\ln\left(\frac{13}{17}\right)\left(\frac{t}{7}\right)} \times \left(\frac{1}{7}\right)\ln\left(\frac{13}{17}\right)$$

$$T'(37.755) = 170e^{\ln\left(\frac{13}{17}\right)\left(\frac{37.755}{7}\right)} \times \left(\frac{1}{7}\right)\ln\left(\frac{13}{17}\right) \approx -1.53$$

The rate of change of the engine's temperature is approximately -1.53°C/min when the temperature of the engine reaches 70°C.

31. 1136

Step 1

Determine an exponential function that models the population's growth.

Use a function of the form $f(t) = Ae^{kt}$ to describe exponential growth, where $f(t)$ is the population after time t, A is the initial population, and k is a constant to be determined from the given information.

Solve for A.

At $t = 0$, the population is 45 000.

$$f(0) = Ae^{0k}$$
$$45\,000 = A$$

After 35 years, the population of the city has grown to 70 000. Therefore, $f(35) = 70\,000$.

Solve for k.

$$f(t) = 45\,000e^{kt}$$
$$70\,000 = 45\,000e^{k(35)}$$
$$\frac{14}{9} = e^{35k}$$
$$\ln\left(\frac{14}{9}\right) = \ln e^{35k}$$
$$\ln\left(\frac{14}{9}\right) = 35k$$
$$\frac{1}{35}\ln\left(\frac{14}{9}\right) = k$$

Therefore, the exponential function is

$$f(t) = 45\,000e^{\ln\left(\frac{14}{9}\right)\left(\frac{t}{35}\right)}.$$

Step 2

Determine when the population will reach 90 000. Set the function $f(t) = 90\,000$, and solve for t.

$$f(t) = 45\,000e^{\ln\left(\frac{14}{9}\right)\left(\frac{t}{35}\right)}$$
$$90\,000 = 45\,000e^{\ln\left(\frac{14}{9}\right)\left(\frac{t}{35}\right)}$$
$$2 = e^{\ln\left(\frac{14}{9}\right)\left(\frac{t}{35}\right)}$$
$$\ln 2 = \ln\left(\frac{14}{9}\right)\left(\frac{t}{35}\right)$$
$$\frac{\ln 2}{\ln\left(\frac{14}{9}\right)} = \frac{t}{35}$$
$$\frac{35\ln 2}{\ln\left(\frac{14}{9}\right)} = t$$
$$54.908 \approx t$$

The population will reach 90 000 after approximately 54.908 years.

Step 3

To determine the rate of population increase when the population reaches 90 000, determine the derivative, $f'(t)$, and evaluate for $t = 54.908$.

$$f(t) = 45\,000e^{\ln\left(\frac{14}{9}\right)\left(\frac{t}{35}\right)}$$

$$f'(t) = \left(45\,000e^{\ln\left(\frac{14}{9}\right)\left(\frac{t}{35}\right)} \times \left(\frac{1}{35}\right)\ln\left(\frac{14}{9}\right)\right)$$

$$f'(54.908) = \left(45\,000e^{\ln\left(\frac{14}{9}\right)\left(\frac{54.908}{35}\right)} \times \left(\frac{1}{35}\right)\ln\left(\frac{14}{9}\right)\right) \approx 1\,136$$

When the population reaches 90 000 in 54.908 years, the rate of population increase will be approximately 1 136 people/yr.

32. WR

Step 1

Determine an exponential function that models the decay of the reactive substance.

When the time is equal to zero, there is 84 kg of the substance.

Solve for A.

$$f(t) = Ae^{kt}$$
$$f(0) = Ae^{0k}$$
$$84 = A$$

The half-life of the substance is 6 months.

This means it takes 6 months for the substance to decrease to half its initial amount. Therefore, $f(6) = 42$.

Solve for k.

$$f(t) = 84e^{kt}$$
$$42 = 84e^{k(6)}$$
$$\frac{1}{2} = e^{6k}$$
$$\ln\left(\frac{1}{2}\right) = 6k$$
$$\frac{1}{6}\ln\left(2^{-1}\right) = k$$
$$-\frac{1}{6}\ln 2 = k$$

Therefore, the exponential function to work with is

$$f(t) = 84e^{-\ln 2\left(\frac{t}{6}\right)}.$$

Step 2

Find the first derivative of the function $f(t)$.

$$f(t) = 84e^{-\ln 2\left(\frac{t}{6}\right)}$$
$$f'(t) = 84e^{-\ln 2\left(\frac{t}{6}\right)}\left(-\frac{1}{6}\ln 2\right)$$

Solve for t when $f'(t) = -7$.

$$f'(t) = 84e^{-\ln 2\left(\frac{t}{6}\right)}\left(-\frac{1}{6}\ln 2\right)$$
$$-7 = 84e^{-\ln 2\left(\frac{t}{6}\right)}\left(-\frac{1}{6}\ln 2\right)$$
$$\frac{-7}{84\left(-\frac{1}{6}\ln 2\right)} = e^{-\ln 2\left(\frac{t}{6}\right)}$$
$$\frac{-7}{-14\ln 2} = e^{-\ln 2\left(\frac{t}{6}\right)}$$
$$\frac{1}{2\ln 2} = e^{-\ln 2\left(\frac{t}{6}\right)}$$
$$\ln\left(\frac{1}{2\ln 2}\right) = -\ln 2\left(\frac{t}{6}\right)$$
$$\frac{\ln\left(\frac{1}{2\ln 2}\right)}{-\ln 2} = \frac{t}{6}$$
$$\frac{6\ln\left(\frac{1}{2\ln 2}\right)}{-\ln 2} = t$$
$$2.8 \approx t$$

The rate of decrease in mass will reach 7 kg/month after approximately 2.8 months.

Geometry and Algebra of Vectors

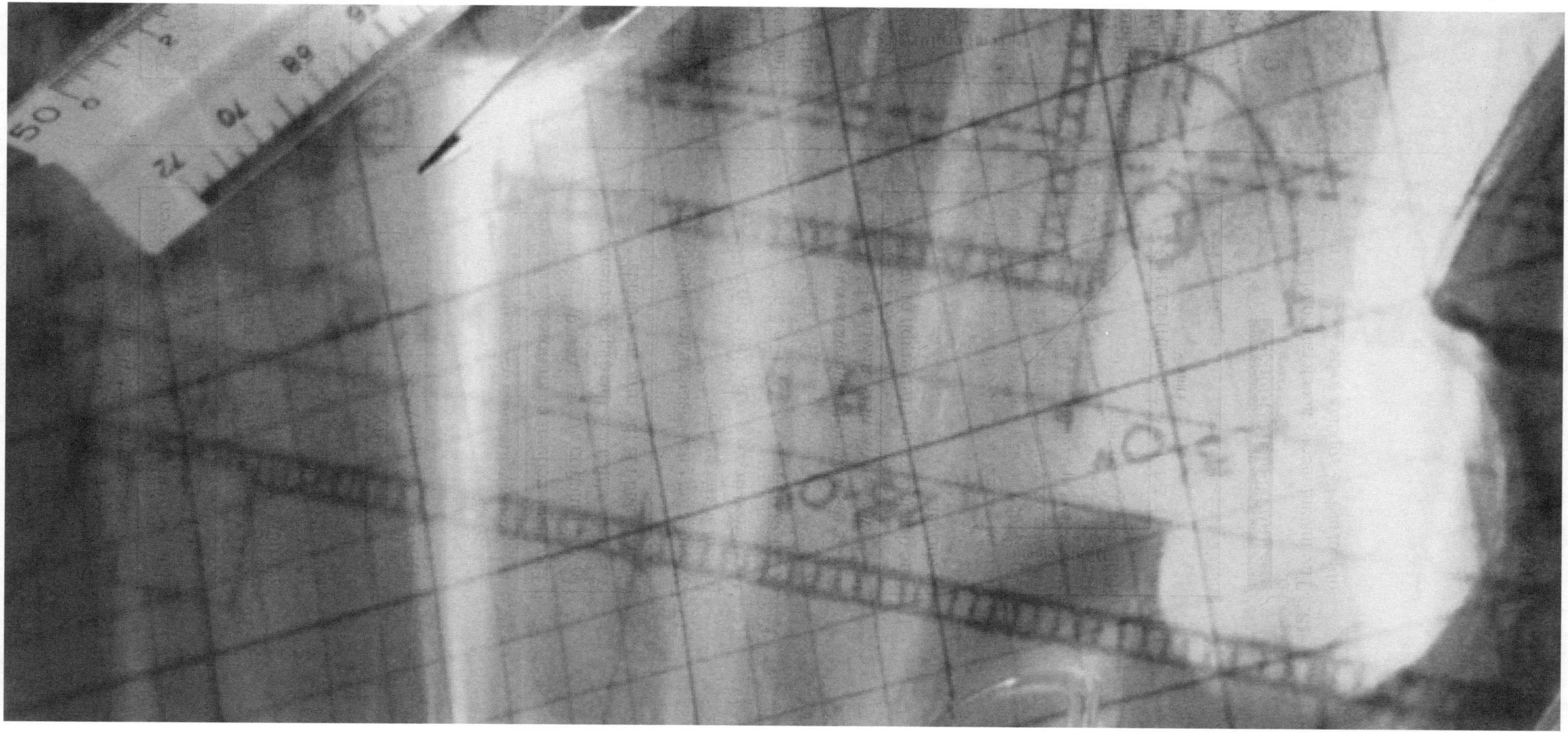

Geometry and Algebra of Vectors

Table of Correlations

Outcome		Practice Questions	Unit Test Questions	Practice Test 1	Practice Test 2
VEC1.0	Representing Vectors Geometrically and Algebraically				
VEC1.1	*recognize a vector as a quantity with both magnitude and direction, and identify, gather, and interpret information about real-world applications of vectors (e.g., displacement, forces involved in structural design, simple animation of computer graphics, velocity determined using GPS)*	1, 2	1, 2		29
VEC1.2	*represent a vector in two-space geometrically as a directed line segment, with directions expressed in different ways (e.g., 320°; N 40° W), and algebraically (e.g., using Cartesian coordinates; using polar coordinates), and recognize vectors with the same magnitude and direction but different positions as equal vectors*	3, 4	3	31	
VEC1.3	*determine, using trigonometric relationships, the Cartesian representation of a vector in two-space given as a directed line segment, or the representation as a directed line segment of a vector in two-space given in Cartesian form x*	5	4	32	30
VEC1.4	*recognize that points and vectors in three-space can both be represented using Cartesian coordinates, and determine the distance between two points and the magnitude of a vector using their Cartesian representations*	6, 7	5, 6		
VEC2.0	Operating With Vectors				
VEC2.1	*perform the operations of addition, subtraction, and scalar multiplication on vectors represented as directed line segments in two-space, and on vectors represented in Cartesian form in two-space and three-space*	8, 9, 10	7, 8, 9	33	31
VEC2.2	*determine, through investigation with and without technology, some properties (e.g., commutative, associative, and distributive properties) of the operations of addition, subtraction, and scalar multiplication of vectors*	11			
VEC2.3	*solve problems involving the addition, subtraction, and scalar multiplication of vectors, including problems arising from real-world applications*	12a, 12b, 13a, 13b	10a, 10b, 11	34a, 34b	32
VEC2.4	*perform the operation of dot product on two vectors represented as directed line segments (i.e., using vector a – vector b = vector ab cosine θ) and in Cartesian form (i.e., using vector a – vector b = a^1b^1 plus a^2b^2 or vector a minus vector b equals a^1b^1 plus a^2b^2 plus a^3b^3) in two-space and three-space, and describe applications of the dot product (e.g., determining the angle between two vectors; determining the projection of one vector onto another)*	14, 15	12, 13		33
VEC2.5	*determine, through investigation, properties of the dot product (e.g., investigate whether it is commutative, distributive, or associative; investigate the dot product of a vector with itself and the dot product of orthogonal vectors)*		14		

VEC2.6	*perform the operation of cross product on two vectors represented in Cartesian form in three-space [i.e., using vector a x vector b = $(a^2b^3 - a^3b^2, a^3b^1 - a^1b^3, a^1b^2 - a^2b^1)$], determine the magnitude of the cross product (i.e., using | vector a x vector b | = | vector a | | vector b | sin θ), and describe applications of the cross product (e.g., determining a vector orthogonal to two given vectors; determining the turning effect [or torque] when a force is applied to a wrench at different angles)*	18, 19	16a, 16b, 16c	36, 37	35
VEC2.7	*determine, through investigation, properties of the cross product (e.g., investigate whether it is commutative, distributive, or associative; investigate the cross product of collinear vectors)*	20	17		
VEC2.8	*solve problems involving dot product and cross product (e.g., determining projections, the area of a parallelogram, the volume of a parallelepiped), including problems arising from real-world applications (e.g., determining work, torque, ground speed, velocity, force)*	16a, 16b, 16c, 17, 21	15, 18, 19	35, 38	34, 36a, 36b
VEC3.0	Describing Lines and Planes Using Linear Equations				
VEC3.1	*recognize that the solution points (x, y) in two-space of a single linear equation in two variables form a line and that the solution points (x, y) in two-space of a system of two linear equations in two variables determine the point of intersection of two lines, if the lines are not coincident or parallel*	22	20	39	37
VEC3.2	*determine, through investigation with technology (i.e., 3-D graphing software) and without technology, that the solution points (x, y, z) in three-space of a single linear equation in three variables form a plane and that the solution points (x, y, z) in three-space of a system of two linear equations in three variables form the line of intersection of two planes, if the planes are not coincident or parallel*	23, 24	21, 22	40	38
VEC3.3	*determine, through investigation using a variety of tools and strategies (e.g., modelling with cardboard sheets and drinking straws; sketching on isometric graph paper), different geometric configurations of combinations of up to three lines and/or planes in three-space (e.g., two skew lines, three parallel planes, two intersecting planes, an intersecting line and plane); organize the configurations based on whether they intersect and, if so, how they intersect (i.e., in a point, in a line, in a plane)*	25	37	47	
VEC4.0	Describing Lines and Planes Using Scalar, Vector, and Parametric Equations				
VEC4.1	*recognize a scalar equation for a line in two-space to be an equation of the form Ax + By + C = 0, represent a line in two-space using a vector equation (i.e., vector r = vector r 0 + t vector m.) and parametric equations, and make connections between a scalar equation, a vector equation, and parametric equations of a line in two-space*	26	23, 24	41a, 41b	39
VEC4.2	*recognize that a line in three-space cannot be represented by a scalar equation, and represent a line in three-space using the scalar equations of two intersecting planes and using vector and parametric equations (e.g., given a direction vector and a point on the line, or given two points on the line)*	27, 28	25, 26	42	40
VEC4.3	*recognize a normal to a plane geometrically (i.e., as a vector perpendicular to the plane) and algebraically, and determine, through investigation, some geometric properties of the plane (e.g., the direction of any normal to a plane is constant; all scalar multiples of a normal to a plane are also normals to that plane; three non-collinear points determine a plane; the resultant, or sum, of any two vectors in a plane also lies in the plane)*	29, 30a, 30b	27, 28	43	

VEC4.4	*recognize a scalar equation for a plane in three-space to be an equation of the form $Ax + By + Cz + D = 0$ whose solution points make up the plane, determine the intersection of three planes represented using scalar equations by solving a system of three linear equations in three unknowns algebraically (e.g., by using elimination or substitution), and make connections between the algebraic solution and the geometric configuration of the three planes*	31, 32	29, 30		41
VEC4.5	*determine, using properties of a plane, the scalar, vector, and parametric equations of a plane*	33, 34	31, 32	44	42
VEC4.6	*determine the equation of a plane in its scalar, vector, or parametric form, given another of these forms*	35, 36	33, 34	45	43
VEC4.7	*solve problems relating to lines and planes in three-space that are represented in a variety of ways (e.g., scalar, vector, parametric equations) and involving distances (e.g., between a point and a plane; between two skew lines) or intersections (e.g., of two lines, of a line and a plane), and interpret the result geometrically*	37, 38	35, 36a, 36b	46	44